John Drayton

Letters Written During a Tour Through the Northern and Eastern

States of America

John Drayton

Letters Written During a Tour Through the Northern and Eastern States of America

ISBN/EAN: 9783744704328

Printed in Europe, USA, Canada, Australia, Japan

Cover: Foto ©Andreas Hilbeck / pixelio.de

More available books at **www.hansebooks.com**

LETTERS
WRITTEN DURING
A TOUR
THROUGH THE
NORTHERN AND EASTERN STATES
OF
AMERICA;

By JOHN DRAYTON.

The scenes of Bufinefs tell us—" What are Men:"
The scenes of Pleafure——" What is all befide."

YOUNG'S NIGHT THOUGHTS.

CHARLESTON: SOUTH-CAROLINA,
PRINTED BY HARRISON AND BOWEN.

M,DCC,XCIV.

PREFACE.

NOTHING is more common, at the first commencement of a young author's career, than to solicit the public favor; and if possible, thereby to support a work, perhaps unworthy of their patronage. But however that custom may have been in use, I cannot in justice to my own feelings, or confistently with the respect which I owe the subscribers to this work in particular, and the public in general, do otherwise, than present it to them liable to any liberal criticism, which its incorrections may occasion.

When

PREFACE.

WHEN I first began, the letters which compose it; their publication was the farthest from my thoughts. My then inducement, was as much the tribute of friendship to an absent acquaintance, as a source of pleasure to myself; in thus filling up, the many leisure moments of a traveller's time, which are otherwise thrown away upon the excesses of a town, or the ruin of a gaming table. I had no plan; but freely wrote from the impulse of the moment, as circumstances permitted, or subjects were occasionally afforded me. Hence, those who expect a critical and exact description of persons, places and things will be disappointed. For it was not a catalogue of things, or a journal of daily occurrences, which I committed to paper; it was the images impressed on

PREFACE.

me refpecting public occurrences, which I wifhed to preferve. I therefore noted them; as well for the refrefhment of my own memory, as to afford me in fome meafure an honorable acquittal as to the ufe of my time, to thofe of my friends, who had favored me with letters of introduction.

THE delay of publifhing this work, renders fome excufe neceffary. Unqueftionably, I ought to have given it to the world fooner: it was my duty to have done fo—and, had it depended only upon me; in this, no difappointment would have taken place. But fo great was the fcarcity of paper, that for a length of time every endeavor to obtain it, was rendered ineffectual. Nor is that which is now ufed, as

good

PREFACE.

good as was intended; all that can be said in its favor is, that it is the best which could be obtained.

As Mr. Genet is now recalled, and another minister substituted in his place; the strictures respecting him would have been omitted, could that have been done with consistency. But, as the public were promised this conclusion to the work, they shall not be disappointed: however mal à propos it may come forward at this late day. And, except the addition of some few notes; the text is presented such as was intended for publication in November last.

Charleston, October 6, 1794.

LIST OF SUBSCRIBERS.

A.
William Anderson, of Cambridge.
Charles James Air.
David Alexander, two copies.
Oliver Alden.

B.
John Bull.
Francis Bremar.
Samuel Brailsford.
James Burn, of St. Jame's Santee.
John Beale.
Thomas W. Bacot.
James Bulgin, two copies.
William Blacklock.
T. B. Bowen, two copies.
William Brailsford.
Benjamin Bayley.
Malcom Brown.
John Bounetheau.
Elihu Hall Bay, one of the judges of the Court of Common Pleas.

SUBSCRIBERS NAMES.

C.

Charles B. Cochran.
Archibald Campbell.
John Cockle.
E. Coffin.
John Crawford.
Samuel Corbett.
James Charles.
William Carfon.
H. Courtney
George Chifolm.

D.

Ifaac Motte Dart.
Jacob Drayton.
William Allen Deas, two copies.
Thomas Doughty.
Henry Deas.
Edward Darrell, jun.
J. Deveaux, Jun.

E.

John Edwards, two copies.
Robert Ellifon, of Cheraws.

F.

Lewis Fogartie.
William Falconer, of Cheraws.
Peter Freneau, two copies.

SUBSCRIBERS NAMES.

James Frafer.
George Forreft.
Thomas Hunter Forreft.
James Futerell.
Walter Forfyth.

G.

Alexander Garden.
William Hafell Gibbes.
Hary Grant.
John Geyer.
Adam Gilchrift.
Robert Gibfon.
Thomas Gibfon.

H.

John Huger.
William Hort, two copies.
D. L. Huger,
John James Haig, of Orangeburgh diftrict.
Richard Hutfon.
George Henderfon.
James Hickey.
Mrs. Sarah Hopton,
Dominick Auguftine Hall.
Jofhua Hargreaves, two copies.
E. Horry.
Elias Lynch Horry.

O

James O'Hear.
Nathaniel Wm. Otis

P

Charles Cotefworth Pinckney, major-general, two copies
Jofeph Peace.
Richard Henry Peyton.
Ezekiel Pickens.
John Parker, fen. of Goofe-creek.
Wm. M. Parker.
Samuel Prioleau, jun. two copies.
Thomas Parker.
John Price, two copies.
William Price, two copies.
William Preftman.
H. Purcell.

R

Edward Rutledge, major, two copies.
David Ramfay.
James B. Richardfon of Camden diftrict.
Edward Rutledge, jun. two copies.
John Rutledge, jun.
Nathaniel Ruffell, two copies.
Alexander Rofs.
Hugh Rofe, two copies.

Peter Roberts.
William Roufe.

S.

Rev. Robert Smith,
General Benjamin Smith, of Belvedere.
B. B. Smith.
Thomas Somarfal, two copies.
William Scott, jun.
Thomas R. Smith two copies.
James Shoolbred.
Thomas Stewart, four copies.
William Simpfon, two copies.
Alexander Shivas.
James Scot.
William Shirtliff.
E. Smerdon
James Smith.
David Sarzedas.
Thomas Wm. Satterthwaite, two copies.
Wm. S Smith
Jervis H. Stevens

T.

Anthony Toomer, two copies.
Simeon Theus.
Lewis Trezevant.
John Taylor, of Columbia.

SUBSCRIBERS NAMES.

Paul Trapier, of Georgetown.
James Thens, two copies.
Adam Tunno, four copies.
George Taylor, two copies.
E. Thayer.
Alaxander Tweed.

V.
Arnoldus Vanderhorst, lieut. col.

W.
John Ward, twelve copies.
Felix Warley.
Daniel Ward.
Thomas Waring, of St. George's Parish.
Samuel Warren, of St. James's, Santee.
Samuel Wigfall, of do.
Elisha Woodard, of Cheraw hill.
T. W. West, two copies.
Thomas Waties, one of the judges of the court of Common Pleas.

ERRATA.

Page.	Line.	
8.	1.	For the one the right, read the one on the right.
12.	2.	For Rout, read Route.
60.	10.	For Which, read Whom.
86.	9	For Earth, read Castle.
105.	86.	For Inforced, read Enforced.
128.	19.	For Majic, read Magic.

A

TOUR, &c.

LETTER I.

A description of the entrance to New-York; in which mention is made of Mr. Bingham's country seat.

New-York, June 15, 1793.

MY DEAR SIR,

ALTHOUGH separated from you by countries, which present a change of climate and of manners, yet believe me, I still indulge the most pleasing remembrance of an absent friend: and with transport do I reflect, that writing affords me an opportunity of still enjoying your
sentiments,

sentiments, and of informing you of mine. With satisfaction, shall some of my hours be devoted to this sweet tribute of friendship: and when joy shall smile around my dwelling, or melancholy bend my head in pensive thought; I will not forget him, with whom I have been accustomed to share them both.

I HAVE at length, arrived at this place; where, the first thing which possesses my mind, is with soft regret to remember those from whom I am now separated. Affections, or friendships, are never so tried, as when absence removes from the sight those, who are their object. Then, and not until then, is every passion alive; and each interview, recalled with fond remembrance to the imagination. And, while the heart throbs with pleasure at former bliss; it heaves with fearful anxiety; lest some untoward accident should sink the soul with sorrow, or follow the complaining pen with unavailing tears. But thank heaven, I have nothing to inform you which can be the cause of pain: matters, which

have

have made a pleafing impreffion upon me fince my departure, fhall alone at prefent be the fubject of recital. I will inform you, that after feven days agreeable failing, we made the land, in the neighbourhood of the inlet to this city. It was the Jerfey fhore, to the fouthward of Sandy-Hook: and foon after we came in view of the high land of Never-fink. Prefenting a variety of profpect, which with a Carolinean accuftomed to a level country, was particularly pleafing.

IMAGINE to yourfelf the Atlantic bounded on the left, by a yellow and bold beach, as you are failing immediately for the entrance into New-York; where, the hills rife immediately from the fhore to a confiderable height: imagine the vallies, and hills, in fpots cleared by the hand of induftry; fome parts of which, where the vegetation was brought forward, prefented to the eye a beautiful carpet of differently coloured greens; while others, newly turned up by the plough were tinged with a beautiful
brown;

brown: and you will have some idea of a prospect, which is still fresh in my memory. Immediately in view of the highest part of the high lands, and within a small distance of them, is a seat of Mr. Bingham's: which affords a beautiful prospect *. It is retired about a mile from the shore; from its high situation overlooks the lands before it, and is bounded only by the distant horison. On its right, the Jersey shore extends as far as the eye can see; wooded with oak and hickory: and on the left are the high lands of Never-sink, rising high above the waters in gentle majesty. Within musket shot of this beautiful shore did we sail, without any danger of accidents. For no breakers foaming over shoals, here terrify the sight: but deep water, and a shore where the sea barely murmured along its bound, seemed to invite us near this agreeable sojourn.

FROM

N O T E.

* Within sight of this place, the engagement was fought by the Ambuscade and Boston frigates.

From the base of these high lands a neck of land called Sandy-hook, runs out into the sea, for about half a mile, making an obtuse angle: and forming within its embrace on one side, and Staten island on the other a beautiful bay. It is very narrow; and upon it an handsome light-house is built, for the direction of vessels. Crossing this bay, we arrived at the entrance to New York: formed by Staten-island on the south, and by Long-island on the north. Where, on either island, hill and valley, meadows and farms present themselves to the enraptured sight. Soon, we passed the narrows.—Called so, because the high lands of Staten and Long-islands, approach each other so much as to make the passage way not more than a mile wide. Here, during the American war forts were constructed; whose guns could shoot with certainty, from shore, to shore. And now, at the distance of four leagues, the city of New-York stretches into sight.

Before arriving at it, we passed three small islands; which chequer the prospect with beautiful

tiful variety. The one the right, contains about thirty acres of ground; has some handsome elevations upon it, as well as some houses; it is called the governor's island: custom having given him the privilege of receiving the rents accruing from it. The other two islands, are on the left. The first of them, contains about fifteen acres of ground, rising gradually from the water to a beautiful elevation in the centre: it is covered with verdure, and crowned with an handsome villa shaded by a few trees. The other, is a small island; upon which, there are several houses: which, from the lowness of the land, seem almost to be built in the water.

After passing these islands, we came opposite the battery; which is at the extreme point of the town: and is situated much like that, which was at White Point at Charleston. It has no merlons, or embrasures; but the guns (which are thirteen in number) are placed upon carriages on a stone platform *en barbette*, some few feet above the level of the water.

water. Between the guns, and the water is a public walk; made by a gentle decline from the platform: and going round the ground upon which the battery is placed. Some little diftance behind the guns, two rows of elm trees are planted; which in a fhort time will afford an agreeable fhade. The flag ftaff rifes from the midft of a ftone tower, and is decorated on the top with a golden ball: and the back part of the ground is laid out in fmaller walks, terraces, and a bowling green.— Immediately behind this, and overlooking it, is the government houfe; built at the expence of the ftate. Then in the back ground, was the city of New-York, crowded with excellent buildings: and its wharves lined with fhipping, and with people. For the day being Sunday, the inhabitants were naturally invited to the waters edge; as well for pleafure, as excited by curiofity.

JUDGE then, what were my fenfations in failing up to this city—where, nature, population, and

and art, had with a generous hand spread so great a collection of beauties before the eye. I was enraptured with the scene. And would you believe me when I say, a wish escaped from me, that I had lived at New-York? It did: But I soon recalled the wanderer home, and flew in imagination to Carolina: there, to throw in my small exertions for my country's good: to which, however imperceptible the thread which binds me may be, my actions for its prosperity shall ever tend. And I trust, as long as nature speeds the blood warm from my heart, shall make me true to her interests in politics, and attached to her by undivided affection. For, within her embrace are contained, almost all which is dear to me in this life. Let my hopes, which are but moderate, but which are pure; be smiled upon by favoring heaven. Let me enjoy the friendship with you, which chance has formed, but which reflection has approved—and I shall have reason to bless my native land. And with encircling friends at my return take pleasure to smile

away

away the day, satisfied with the meridian of Carolina,

LETTER

LETTER II.

An account of the City of New-York. Its commerce and public buildings. Its library and museum. Its public amusements. The happy situation of the state of New-York respecting taxes, contrasted with that of South-Carolina.

New-York, June 25, 1793.

TO-MORROW, I propose leaving this place, on my rout for Boston: and my stay here, contrary to my original determination, gives me a lesson of which I shall be mindful in future. Which is, never to resolve to leave a place at a certain time; where, the hospitality of its inhabitants may persuade one to the contrary. That, has been my case. Having met with unexpected attentions from families and persons, to whom, I had no letters: and whose acquaintance was not to be obtained but by a short stay. This, was my reason for not pursuing my destination: it not through a fickleness

of

of difpofition, or in a wild purfuit of pleafure. And this ftay, furnifhes me with the means, as well as the opportunity, of once more addreff- ing you before my departure: and of giving fome account of the city of New-York. Firft premifing, that you muft not expect more par- ticulars, than you may imagine in the courfe of a fortnight, with reafonable enquiries and ob- fervations, I may have obtained.

It claims a fuperiority of fituation as a com- mercial city, to any on the continent. Retir- ed, about eight leagues from the fea; in half a tide, veffels from thence may be moored at its wharves. It is built at the extreme end of New-York ifland, at the confluence of the Hud- fon and Eaft rivers: and in pofition is much like that of Charlefton. On the fouth of it, runs the Hudfon, fome hundred miles; thro' the ftates of New-York, New-Jerfey, and at the back of Connecticut and Vermont; until it waftes itfelf in the country between the lakes Ontario, and Champlain. It is the boundary between the ftates of Jerfey and New-York;

and

and the channel of great wealth to that city. Up this river, British forty gun ships have sailed some distance. Upon the border of it, was Arnold's and Andre's plot carried on : and its bosom (which had it been sensible, would have shrunk from such a weight of infamy) received the traitor in his escape to New-York. On the northern side, is East river ; famous for having hell-gate on it. We shall pass it to-morrow. No Sibyl guiding our course as Æneas had ;* however, I hope not to be less fortunate. This river communicates with the sound, running between Long-Island and the state of Connecticut : and leads much of the commerce of Rhode-Island and Connecticut to this city.

The greater part of its wharves, are built upon East river : and there, the trade of the city is principally carried on. It is said to contain

N O T E.

*Ibant obscuri solâ sub nocte per umbram, Perque domos Ditis vacuas, et inania regna.

Virg.

tain thirty thoufand inhabitants; and is crowded with ftores and fhops: the moft of which are in the retail line, though many of them are in the wholefale bufinefs. Quite like an European town, there are few articles which may not be here obtained: and that cheaper, than in Carolina. How to account for this, I am at a lofs: but believe it may in fome meafure be owing, to property in veffels, more punctuality in payments, and fhorter credits. Almoft every merchant, has a property in fhipping: hence, in proportion as he gains by the freight, he can afford to reduce the price of his goods. And is not driven to the neceffity of putting an additional advance upon them, in order to compenfate for the expenfe of freight; unavoidably incurred by the employ of a foreign bottom. The common time of crediting the farmers, is fix months. Added to this, people in a bufy line of life, are fatisfied to live comfortably: and do not endeavour to equal their neighbours in fhow, whofe good fortune it is to enjoy more eafy circumftances. Thus, having fewer wants to gratify, they can afford to fell cheap: and although fometimes they may be

flow

flow in amaſſing a fortune, yet in the end they are more ſure of enjoying a comfortable and independent living. Induſtry, appears as the leading character among the catalogue of their virtues. It directs them to purſuits, where an harmony of action adds happineſs to the individual; and rejoices him to ſee founded thereon, the ſtrength of his country. In honeſt occupations perhaps no Americans are more attentive: whether we view them as relating to perſeverance, or ingenuity. And I never ſaw the latter more tried, than in a conteſt between two public vendue criers: which, one day, arreſted my attention in the ſtreets.

BESIDES having a flag, denoting it to be auction day, the vendue maſters employ public criers: for the expreſs purpoſe of perſuading people to attend the ſale. They walk before the door of the auction room, and ſtrive by all the power of their eloquence, to catch the attention of the paſſing crowd. Seeing two of theſe ſtreet orators, from oppoſite ſides of the ſtreet endeavouring to rally perſons around their reſpective colours;

colours; the contrast of person observable in them induced me to stop for a moment, and observe the effect which it produced. The one, appeared to be a cold, phlegmatic character; the other, a lively, good looking person. The first, had a routine of language, which he dealt out mechanically, and with much vociferation. The other, with a brisk lively deportment, while he informed the public what was going on within doors, lost no opportunity of mixing the dulce cum utile. He spared his lungs, when he perceived no body coming that way: but when any advances were made towards him, he spoke, he sang, he looked pleasant, he laughed at his opponent; and in many cases, finally carried his point. Whether it were that his auction room were in better request, or that his mode of invitation were more agreeable; certain it is, that he attracted a greater number of customers, than his unmoving rival. And such an advantage, will lively and sensible characters ever have over those, who want elasticity in their composition. They catch the public attention, by their manners; and per-

suade

suade the mind to notice the subject of discussion.

From eleven to two o'clock, the merchants, brokers, &c. meet at the Tontine coffee-house, in Wall-street; where, they transact all their concerns in a large way, and where, the politics of the day are considered. This, is a most convenient, and large building; having an elegant suit of rooms, bath, and other conveniencies. Here, the insurance offices are kept: blank checks on the different banks, are ready for those who may want them, and every thing in the busy line transacted. When the Ambuscade frigate was here, there was a vast throng in this house, every evening. It consisted of two parties, and was productive of much opposition of sentiment; which, I believe would ere long have brought them to extremities, had not the cap of liberty, with a motto on it of "*Sacred to Liberty*," been fixed up in the coffee room; where, it now is. This, quieted the minds as well of the one party, as the other: and sent to attend upon their family concerns

concerns many men, who were better employed at home, than in the difcuffion of politics.

The ftreets of the city are all paved with round ftones, except on the fides: where, they are generally paved with brick, or flat ftones. They are irregular. Some, of them being ftraight; fome, forming almoft a bend of half a circle; others, cutting them acutely; others, forking, and making a triangular area of houfes. One part of a ftreet, may be wide enough for feveral carriages to pafs; while another part of it, admits only two with difficulty. The beft ftreets in it are Broad-way, Broad-ftreet, Queen-ftreet, and Wall-ftreet. But notwithftanding this irregularity, there is fomething extremely agreeable in the appearance of the town. The irregularities themfelves, tend to make it fo; particularly the curves in fome of the ftreets: which, confequently do not give the full profpect at once; but by degrees unfold it to the view. It is in this way, that Federal-hall opens to the fight, as one walks up Broad-ftreet.

At the lower end of Broad-way, is the battery, and public parade; of which, I have already given you some account*: and I now present you with a sketch of it, as seen from this spot. While I was taking it, the Ambuscade sailed by, having a liberty cap on the fore-top-gallant-mast head. I drew it with pleasure, hoping that it would be an ornament to the piece: as I trust every thing, which brings to the mind ideas of social liberty, and good government, will be.

Overlooking this prospect, is the government house; placed upon an handsome elevation, and fronting Broad-way: having before it an elegant illiptical approach, round an area of near an acre of ground, enclosed by an iron railing. In the midst of this is a pedestal, which formerly was pressed by a leaden equestrian statue of the king of Great-Britain: but having been dismantled of that, for the use of the

N O T E.
* See Page 8.

the continental army, it now remains ready, in due time I hope, to receive the ftatue of the Prefident of the United States of America. When that period fhall arrive, in addition to the many daily occurrences which lead the mind of the paffenger to penfive reflection; this monument of his country's gratitude fhall call his attention: and while deeds of former times, fhall pafs in fweet review before him, the tear, fhall lament the lofs of an hero—but the heart collected within itfelf, fhall urge him by fo bright an example, to call forth his powers, and to purfue the fteps of virtue, and of honor*.

A VAST number of houfes have been built in this city, fince the war; fome of which are extremely

N O T E.

* Sed tamen, ex omnibus præmiis virtutis fi effet habenda ratio præmiorum, ampliffimum effe præmium gloriam: effe hanc unam, quæ brevitatem vitæ pofteritatis memoria confolaretur: quæ efficeret, ut abfentes adeffemus, mortui viverimus: hanc denique effe, cujus gradibus etiam homines in cælum videantur afcendere. CIC.

extremely ornamental: and none more so, than the government house. It is two stories high. Projecting before it is a portico, covered by a pediment: upon which is superbly carved in basso relievo the arms of the state, supported by justice and liberty, as large as life. The arms and figures are white, placed in a blue field: and the pediment is supported by four white pillars of the Ionic order, which are the height of both stories.

FEDERAL-HALL, is built upon Wall-street, and fronts Broad-street, in the same manner, as the government house does Broad-way. This, is an elegant and grand building; well adapted for a senatorial presence. Here, I saw portraits of the president, of the secretary of the treasury, and of the present governor of this state; executed by colonel Trumbull as large as life: and as far as I could judge good likenesses. The back ground of the president's portrait, represents a part of New-York; and the British fleet sailing up the narrows. Here, are also a museum, and library. The library contains about five

five thoufand volumes. The mufeum, was fhewn to the worft advantage; being but partially expofed, and that, in a very fmall room.*

At the upper end of Broad-way, fronting an area of three or four acres of ground (which are laid out in public walks, and planted with trees)

N O T E.

* The mufeum has been fince moved from Federal hall to the exchange, at the foot of Broad ftreet : where, it offers a more extenfive gratification to the fpectator. Among its prefent curiofities is the model (in clay) defigned, and executed by the celebrated Italian artift in ftatuary, Mr. Ceracchi, for perpetuating the memory of American liberty. It is made upon a fcale proportioned to one hundred feet in length, and as many feet in height : and for grandeur, and emblematical device, is fuppofed would furpafs any thing of the kind, whether ancient or modern. Nothing, but the expence attending the execution of it, has impeded its progrefs : that being eftimated at forty thoufand guineas.—Perhaps, at fome future day, fhould Mr. Ceracchi be then living, the finances of America may affift the completion of fo happy a defign. Here alfo is to be feen Mr. Bowen's wax-work, in the middle of the mufeum.

trees) are some public buildings; consisting of a bridewell, a poor house, and jail: with its attendant the gallows. The criminal is here partly hidden by a lattice work; which, I am led to believe may have a good tendency: as whether the culprit dies bravely or like a coward, those around are ignorant of it. The mob goes away, not enlarging upon the fortitude of his death: but commenting upon the certainty of his punishment. And thence, drawing instruction for

N O T E.

seum. Among which, are those of Alexander Hamilton, secretary of the treasury of the United States, Dr. Franklin, and John Hancock, late governor of the commonwealth of Massachusetts. These, with the rest of the collection, are now placed with an happy taste in a room sixty feet, by thirty: with an arched ceiling of twenty feet high.

The building in which this museum is kept, was formerly the public resort of merchants; and has been long built. It is supported on arcades, and is ornamented with a cupola; on the top of which in regal times a crown was placed. But that now lies neglected, and almost unnoticed in a corner of the museum; giving way to the more pleasing decoration of a liberty cap.

for a moral conduct; not encouragement in a vicious one.

NEAR thefe buildings is an hofpital, capable of containing a large number of invalids : and fome little diftance from it is the college ; where about eighty ftudents are at prefent. They have their ftudies in the college, but are boarded out in the city. In addition to the improvement acquired here common to the claffes of a college, lectures upon anatomy, chymiftry, and other branches appertaining to furgery and phyfic, are delivered under the direction of the college; and I am informed there are about thirty ftudents who now attend them.

SCARCELY out of the city, is a very good fhip-yard, fituated upon Eaft river. Yefterday, a fhip capable of carrying nine hundred barrels of rice, was launched from it : and feveral more are upon the ftocks, one of which is to be an Indiaman. While fpeaking of fhipping permit me to mention, that lee-boards are

very

very much in ufe at this place, with all the fmall floops, and other light boats; particularly with thofe navigating the Hudfon, and attending the ferries. They are a great affiftance to them, in failing clofe upon the wind; and fcem by their ufe, much to meet the public approbation.

I JUST arrived here time enough to be at their concerts, and plays. Their band which is good, has the great addition of Mrs. Pownal's voice; whom I have heard fing at the play, the concert, and at Trinity church (St. John's day.) She may with truth, be confidered as a good performer. And although the reverend divine at church, feemed to deliver himfelf with much earneftnefs; yet fuch was the crowd, that the voice of Mrs. Pownal alone, arrefted attention; and claimed the privilege of being heard. She is advanced in years; came over from England laft fall; and ftill retains vaft powers in vocal mufic. The company of actors acquit themfelves very well, and do not ftand in need of much prompting; -
which.

which, is an advantage they have over many in the fame line of life.

Good hackney-coaches, phætons or other carriages may now be hired at New-York; it is neceffary however to give fome little previous notice, as they are kept at no public ftand; but only at the houfes of their refpective owners.

The rides in the neighbourhood of the city, are for miles beautiful. Every elevation of ground, prefenting fome handfome country feat.—With what pleafure, have I often viewed them. They were as much mine at thofe moments, as the real poffeffors'. I enjoyed each beauty, as much as they could do: and there was nothing wanting to render my happinefs complete, but the company of thofe who are dear to me.

The ftate of New-York, is certainly in its prefent fituation enviable; for there are fcarcely ly any taxes levied in it. The state has so much money in the funds, that the interest of it, after paying the expences of government, leaves a balance in its favour*. It derives this principally from the confiscations and amercements, which took place in consequence of the American war.

How different, is the situation of Carolina! —In some instances, the state has been obliged to refund the monies received from the sales of confiscated property: in others, to pay the value of the estates sold. Hence, an addition to the exigencies of government. While her citizens, dispirited with their extreme loss of indents;

N O T E.

* Since the period when the above letter was written, the accounts of the United States with the individual states have been adjusted; by which it appears, that the state of New-York is indebted to the United States in the sum of 2,074,846 dollars. And that the United States are indebted to the state of South-Carolina, in the sum of 1,205,978 dollars.

dents; are still obliged to raise the enormous annual tax, of forty thousand pounds sterling; as yet hopeless of any reduction*.

A CONTRAST of this nature, so much to her disadvantage: so much against the prosperity of a country standing high in the page of history, for sufferings during the American war; throws such a gloom upon me, as here to let the curtain fall. Though not without first assuring you of my sincere remembrance.

N O T E.

* THE tax levied in South Carolina for the year 1790, was about £ 24,000 sterling.
1791, 36,000
1792, 40,000
1793, 40,000

LETTER

LETTER III.

A Visit to Fresh-Pond.

Boston, July 3, 1793.

I HAVE been led into these expressions, by making an excursion this afternoon to a place called Fresh-Pond: being about five miles from hence. Where, nature has spread both land and water in soft perspective to delight the eye; and to charm the imagination with improvements which might be made on it. It was there, that I saw and conversed with a maid, whose age, person and manners were as much like one who bears the name of ———, as you may possibly conceive. She went and picked a water-lilly and gave it to me; sweet
pledge

pledge of attention! It now lays on the table before me. Would that I could nourish thee for ever, thou beft emblem of innocence. For, how many foft ideas have fwept over my fond imagination, fince I firft received thee to my protection. But, how are thofe fenfations recalled, quick to a painful point; when I reflect that the faireft forms in nature, and the moft beautiful flowers of the field, muft die. It languifhes, it dies—And like it die all the fublunary profpects of man; leaving not a wreck behind.

It is late; and I am to rife at five to-morrow, for the purpofe of hearing a poem delivered at fix, in honor of the day: which, I make no doubt you will join me in celebrating. May refrefhing repofe prepare us to hail with decent feftivity, and affectionate remembrance, an anniverfary; which, has placed America on a rank with nations: and caufes her to be refpected by the fovereigns of the world.

LETTER

LETTER IV.

The Fourth Day of July—how celebrated at Boston.

Boston, July 7, 1793.

I DID not go to hear the poem on the fourth instant, an accident disappointed me. However, at twelve o'clock of that day, I had the pleasure of hearing an oration delivered in commemoration of the anniversary of American independence: which, afforded me ample compensation.

REMARKABLE for the omission of nothing tending continually to keep alive, principles of patriotism and knowledge; the inhabitants of Boston do not so much celebrate this day by noise, riot, and feasting, as by bringing to the recollection of the old, and spreading to the minds of the young, its collected happiness. The old, are publicly called upon to witness the

the oppreſſion, which was the cauſe of the American revolution. They, are invited to contraſt the preſent ſituation of the country, with former times: and by a bright countenance, and joyful aſſent, to acknowledge how much the change is for the better. The young, are learned the obligations which they owe their parents; who have been inſtrumental in their preſent happineſs. They, become fired with a love of their country, and enthuſiaſts in the cauſe of ſocial liberty.

"Those of you my countrymen (ſaid John
'Quincy Adams,* who delivered the oration
'upon that occaſion) thoſe of you, who were
'actors in thoſe intereſting ſcenes, will beſt
'know, how feeble and impotent is the lan-
'guage of this deſcription, to expreſs the im-
'paſſioned emotions of the ſoul, with which
you

NOTE.

* This gentleman has been ſince appointed miniſter reſident from the United States of America, to their high mightineſſes the ſtates general of the United Netherlands.

'you were then agitated: yet, it were injuftice
'to conclude from thence, or from the greater
'prevalence of private, or perfonal motives in
'thefe days of calm ferenity, that your fons
'have degenerated from the virtues of their fa-
'thers. Let it rather be a fubject of pleafing re-
'flection to you, that the generous and difin-
'terefted energies, which you were fummoned
'to difplay, are permitted by the bountiful in-
'dulgence of Heaven to remain latent in the
'bofoms of your children. From the prefent
'profperous appearance of our public affairs,
'we may admit a rational hope that our coun-
'try will have no occafion to require of us
'thofe extraordinary, and heroic exertions,
'which it was your fortune to exhibit. But
'from the common verfatility of all human def-
'tiny, fhould the profpect hereafter darken,
'and the clouds of public misfortune thicken,
'to a tempeft; fhould the voice of our coun-
'try's calamity ever call us to her relief, we
'fwear by the precious memory of the fages
'who toiled, and of the heroes who bled in
'her defence, that we will prove ourfelves not
'unworthy of the prize, which they fo dearly
purchafed;

' purchased; that we will act as the faithful dif-
' ciples of those who so magnanimously taught
' us the instructive lesson of republican virtue."

Such, were the sentiments that day disseminated among an approving audience, by a
young man, chosen by the townsmen for that
particular occasion. Such, have been the sentiments, which for twenty-two years* have annually roused the citizens to a knowledge of their situation. And such, will be the sentiments, which
for times to come shall I hope arrest their attention; and impress them with the duties of their
several stations.

Should we trace the medium of patriotism,
through all its different stages; and follow it,
from the hordes of savages who roam the wilds
unrestrained by the fetters of law, to where,

we

* Orations have been annually delivered in Massachu-
sett upon the subject of liberty and government, since the
year 1771.

we meet focieties of politenefs and civilization; we will find, that nothing is better calculated to imprefs this ardor patriæ, than the voice of recital and perfuafion, in the face of one's country. The favage, fings the deeds of his fathers: and round the facred fire, encites the young men to glory. In focieties, games, anniverfaries and orations, recal continually to remembrance, the happinefs of the ftate, and the virtues of its deferving citizens. Sweet effence of every noble action, it is to thee, Fame, that virtuous exertions tend. If man were to die, and be forgotten; life, would oftentimes be purchafed, with the lofs of honor. " I will not
' blot and defile that which is paft (fays the illuf-
' trious Sidney) by endeavouring to provide for
' the future. I have ever had in my mind, that
' when God fhould caft me into fuch a condi-
' tion, as that I cannot fave my life, but by doing
' an indecent thing: he fhows me, that the
' time is come, wherein I fhould refign it."

Is there a man, who upon thefe public occafions, when every generous emotion is called
forth

forth, whofe heart doth not glow with feelings too great to tell? Is there one; who doth not then feel the blood fpeed from his heart; fpreading an applauding blufh over his face : while at times, a chill fhoots like lightning over every part of his body : and an honeft pride, fits trembling on his eye?—If there be fuch; he is not born to live with his equals upon earth. His heart, callous to feeling, is fit only to be in the breaft of a tyrant—or to vegetate with the continual drudgery of a flave.*

LETTER

N O T E.

* ———— hic niger eft: hunc tu Romane caveto.

HOR.

LETTER V.

Passage from New-York to Newport. Account of that town. The situation of its commerce. Its public amusements. A ride through the island: affording an account of the face of the country. Passage from Newport, to Providence. Description of the town. Its commerce. Journey from thence to Boston; and the hospitality of its inhabitants.

Boston, July 9, 1793.

MY being in so complaining an humour when I wrote to you on the third instant, hindered me from giving any account of what occurred during my coming hither. Such a disposition at that moment, was the cause of much egotism, which is at no time common with me; but in which I may indulge, when I can trust it to the bosom of a friend. For, herein consists the essence, and happiness of friendship. It is in this communication of sentiments, of pleasures and of pains; of prospects of happiness,

nefs, or impending ftorms of misfortune, that an heart rejoices in an union of fouls. By the commerce of friendfhip, every fweetnefs in life is appretiated: while its foft accents fmooth its uneafy ruggednefs, and meliorate the bitternefs of misfortune.

I went from New-York to Newport in the ftate of Rhode-ifland, by the way of the found; which, runs between Long-ifland and the main, almoft the whole of the way: through the extent of one hundred and fifty miles. The profpects which every where meet the eye, during this jaunt, are very agreeable. The uneavennefs of the ifland, alternately rifing into hills, or finking into vallies; crowned with woods or opening fields of agriculture; are what I am perfuaded would have given you pleafure to have feen. They would have brought to your recollection the place, which it has been my happinefs to name, and your politenefs to call " *the* ' *Profpect*:" and which, I hope now prefents you with an harveft flattering to your wifhes.

There

There is so great an intercourse between the several towns upon this sound, and the city of New-York, that it is consequently crowded with vessels: of which, we generally had in sight fifteen or twenty. Before entering upon the sound, we passed through Hell-gate: serving to strengthen an opinion I had long formed; that obstacles, and dangers in travelling were found always less upon trial, than from the relations of a traveller. Instead of much danger and sublimity of scene, I saw nothing but a strong tide, and rocks scattered along the passage, over which the water rippled. After a sail of twenty-six hours, we arrived at the town of Newport: situated on an island in Narragansct bay: and having before it a quiet and deep harbour, quite protected from winds by a small island which is before the town; upon which there has been a large fort, for its protection. At present, nothing gives it a military appearance, but the flag: the fort, having been entirely dismantled.

The town, is said to contain about seven thousand inhabitants. And I am afraid, is rather

ther in decline, than in profperity. The wrath of kings, fell upon it during the American war; and it felt fo feverely the fcourge of their armies and fleets ; that it will be long ere it fhall recover its former profperity. Befides, it has a more ferious difficulty to contend with, in being rivalled of its commerce by the town of Providence; fituated about ten leagues farther up the country.

THE inhabitants have lately fitted up a room in the form of a theatre, capable of containing about two hundred perfons: much in the ftyle of what *Harmony-hall* was with us. They have a rope-dancer attached to the company, by the name of Placide. I faw him, and his wife, who is an handfome woman, about twenty-two years of age, dance an allemande upon the ftage : in which, their bodies were thrown into a variety of pofitions. Some, wherein the fancy might almoft rage free of controul : others, wherein every elegance of form, was difplayed to an admiring affemblage of fpectators. They feemed to move by mechanifm, fo eafy were their attitudes ;

tudes; and so fine, the union of affection which seemed to produce them.

At this place, is a library house: I wish I could say a library. But that alas! has been taken away, by the pilfering hand of the British. Who in this, as well as in other instances, carried on war not only against men, but against learning. And like the Goths and Vandals, swept every thing before them, which they could possibly do.

I took a ride through the extent of the island, which is about twelve miles long. It is parcelled out every way into small farms, which are divided, and laid out in all directions, by stone walls. There is not much variety in the scene. The eye, is thrown around for trees; but in vain. The zephyrs, have no foliage here, upon which they may dance. For the troops of Britain, like the locusts of Afric, have withered each tree upon this once happy island: and when they departed, left the inhabitants

bitants no fhrubs, under whofe fhade, they might reft themfelves in peace. But their induftry begins to raife up fome trees, to defend them from the fummer fun; though at a great expence, as they have them all to buy. And they have need of them. For never did the lilly and the rofe, call for more protection; than in this fmall ifland. Such complexions are here, as you can only in imagination form; for, you have never feen any thing like them. It is here, that the fenfualift in beauty muft come, to obtain a gratification of his wifhes. It is here, that the painter muft direct his courfe, to copy the greateft excellence of nature. Happy ifland! Happy in holding within your fond embrace, not the leaft perfect of American beauty. Let the winds howl over thy lands, too much unprotected from their mercilefs ravages. Let the fun pour down his moft faturated rays, upon your not the lefs fertile glebe. Let the fogs, impervious even to the fight, hide occafionally the fruit which Pomona offers to your harvefts. Still, wilt thou have this confolation; that here Venus arifes from the

fea,

sea*, to rejoice the wondering eyes of men. Here, she makes the seat of love; and here smiles away the inconveniencies of the day.

AFTER staying at Newport two days, I took my passage on board of a packet for Providence; where, I arrived in three hours and an half. And never in a worse time for observations as a traveller; it being insufferably hot: and the situation of the town rather encreasing it, than otherwise. It is situated on each shore of a narrow river, along the side of the hills down to the waters edge. Where, the summer breezes may blow over it in vain; serving only to tantalize the citizens, with what they cannot enjoy. It is however a flourishing town, and is the present seat of government: having a baptist church with one of the tallest and handsomest steeples in America. It is said to be two hundred and twenty feet high. The church is built of wood, and is elegantly finished in the inside:

N O T E.

* Orta salo, suscepta solo, patre edita Cœlo.   Aus.

inside: being illuminated at night by a superb glass chandelier. The church has been lately repaired and painted at the expence of a Miss B———n; whose fortune furnished her with the means, while her inclination prompted her here to return a portion of those riches, which heaven had given her. And sweet must her feelings be, when she reflects on this good appropriation of what is of no value, but as it assists the pleasures of an honest and well-spent life.

Each part of the town, is connected by a bridge thrown across the river, the whole width of the street. There are foot ways on each side of it, in which three persons may walk abreast: and the carriage way is wide enough for as many carriages to pass at one time. At night it is illuminated by three lamps on each side.

Upon an eminence within the town, and overlooking it, is an handsome and commodious

ous brick college ;* where at prefent numbers of youth are educated. I had not time to go into it, or opportunities of making any particular enquiries refpecting it.

THE town is faid to contain fix thoufand inhabitants: four thoufand lefs than Charlefton. And yet it fends three or four fhips to India in each year! would to heaven, that we were as much advanced in commerce. In comparifon with the trading towns of the northern and eaftern ftates, pardon the expreffion when I fay, thofe of the fouthern are but in leading ftrings. It is a melancholy truth, but neverthelefs proper to be known; becaufe, the knowledge of a weaknefs is the firft ftep towards the taking meafures, for the encreafe of our ftrength. But it may be faid, do we not enjoy every fweet arifing from agriculture? Does it not afford the means of every enjoyment of life? It affords that, which will obtain them; but with

an

NOTE.
* Rhode-Ifland college.

an advance upon goods, which direct importation would save. And that advance not bringing an extra benefit to the merchant; while it lays on an extra expence, upon the planter. One of the best principles in government, is to favor agriculture as the first source of wealth. To favor commerce in such manner, as that while it be nourished by agriculture, it shall not throw unnecessary burdens upon it. If the southern states then, have riches and men to spare, why should not their vessels ride the ocean, making it subservient to their prosperity in as great a degree, as their northern neighbours? Does it require an iron bound soil, or northern latitude, to give birth to extensive commerce? Believe me, it does not. Nothing more is necessary than industry and enterprise, to enable them to draw treasures from the Indies, and commodities from all parts of the world. It is this, which when united with agriculture, will make Carolina truly independent, and place her in a situation enviable among nations.

From Providence to Boston is a journey of forty miles, and the travelling easy; owing to
the

the conveniency of stage coaches. . At the latter place I am arrived; where hospitality seems to be a national virtue. I have been here, since the second day of July, and have never dined at home but twice : and sometimes, have even breakfasted abroad.

I YESTERDAY dined with the select-men of the town, at Faneuil-hall ; but shall defer informing you upon what occasion, until my next letter : this, I make no doubt being sufficiently tiresome. Therefore, shall take my leave at present, continuing my wishes for your health and happiness.

LETTER.

LETTER VI.

An account of the public schools at Boston. A descant upon the blessings which attend patriotism and religion when rightly enjoyed. A contrast between the state of information possessed by the inhabitants of the commonwealth of Massachusetts, and those of S. Carolina.

Boston, July 10, 1793.

I MENTIONED in my last letter, that I dined with the select men of the town, on the 8th instant. It is my intention at present to inform you upon what occasion it was, and what were the occurrences of the day. You must then know, that I had been previously invited by them, to attend the visitation of their public schools on that day. Once, every year, they are visited in this public manner, besides, being attended at other times by a committee; and happy was it for me, that their visitation took place at that auspicious moment.

I

I enjoyed thereby a pleasure, which perhaps I may never receive again in this place.

It is to the honor of Boston, that its youth are almost entirely educated in a public manner; and at the public expence. For this purpose, a proportionate tax is laid upon the citizens sufficient to support schools : where, the poor as well as the rich, have an equal claim to the master's attention, and the benefit of the institution : without any additional expence*. They are here offered by their natural, to their political parent, for the purpose of being educated ; not, as may suit the whim of their relations, but, as may tend most to their country's good. To view these sources of knowledge, to encourage the exertions of the scholars, and to observe the attention of
their

N O T E.

* I have been informed that the expences attending each school in Boston, exclusive of paper, ink and books, are,

Head master,	£.200 that money——	£.155 11 0	sterl.
Usher,	100	—— 77 15 6	
Firing	20 cords of wood		

their masters, was the end of our visitation. A cause, grateful to the feelings of every one who attended them. Never, never, were my feelings more excited, or my affections and pleasures more awakened, than upon this occasion. Often, did the tear, that witness of sensibility spread itself like lightning over mine eyes; and fain would I have indulged so sweet a pleasure: did it not betray a weakness, which, upon public occasions it were better to avoid. Wrapt up in extacy of thought, I forgot that I was young: my affection like that of a parent, embraced all the little ones before me; while my best wishes were offered up for their prosperity.

The procession began at 3 o'clock, A. M. and consisted of the select men of the town, the lieutenant governor*, and other public officers of the commonwealth; The vice-president of

N O T E.
* The governor was too ill to attend.

of the United States of America: the clergy: confuls of foreign powers; refpectable gentlemen of the town; and ftrangers who had been invited: making I fuppofe near one hundred in number. Our vifits were fcarcely finifhed by 3 o'clock P. M. for we went to feven different fchools.—Six, for the attainment of ufeful American knowledge; and the feventh, for that of the claffics.

The fchool rooms are built at the public expence; large enough to accommodate two hundred fcholars; and are oblong. The feats are difpofed along the length of the room, five rows deep on each fide; rifing one above another, and leaving a paffage way in the middle. Each bench is capable of accommodating five fcholars: hence, with a glance of the eye, one may make a tolerably good guefs, at the number which may be prefent. There are generally two of thefe rooms under the fame roof; one below, and the other, above ftairs. The one in the firft floor, is for the education of girls; and the upper one, is for that of boys. Be not

not furprized, at my mentioning that girls are educated in this public manner. It is the pride of the citizens, that it is fo done. They glory in that principle of equality, which directs them here to place their daughters. They reflect with fweet fatisfaction, that here, their youth are trained up to induftry, and focial affection: and are perfuaded that when they grow up, they will never forget thofe early obligations, received from the foftering hands of their country. Sweet fchool for every public virtue!—It was thus, that Greece fowed thofe feeds of patriotifm, which long made her fhine unrivalled, in the hiftory of nations. The acquifition of improvement was encouraged, by prefenting premiums and conferring honorary diftinctions upon thofe who excelled. To gain a prize in the Olympic, Nemean, or Ifthmian games, was what not only individuals, but kings contended for; and upon him in whofe favor the decree was given, not only honor was conferred, but his whole family partook of the glory*.

AND

N O T E.
* Pott. Antiq. Vol. 1ft, page 440.

AND should I be allowed to hazard an opinion respecting American education, I would say, let the youth grow up amidst annual festivals, commemorative of the events of the American war; and sacred to the memory of the worthies, who were sharers of its troubles, and have left the stage of life. " Let them learn to
' weep over their tombs: to bless, and to imi‑
' tate their virtues. Let them know, what hav‑
' ing thus learned, they never can forget; that
' the pride of a free man braves all dangers;
' *but never disturbs the public order* :* that hu‑
' man blood ought to be lavished for liberty,
' but ought to flow for no other cause: that war
' is horrible, if it be unnecessary: that it is the
' reproach of the mercinary, who sells his life
' for gold, or for the detestable honor of cool
' barbarity: but that it consigns to immorta‑
' lity the patriot hero who devotes his life for
 ' his

N O T E.

* IN tranquillo, tempestatem adversam optare, dementis est. Cic.

'his country*." When education hath enlightened their minds, and this amor patriæ hath been fully imprinted on their hearts, then, and not until then, may thofe whofe circumftances permit, vifit foreign countries. Their connexions, will by that time be formed; and foreign prejudices will not be likely to affect their judgments. Departing, not ignorant of their country's interefts, they will be prepared by juft contrafts of manners, government and politics, to render it fervices at their return, and to heap honors upon themfelves.

CHILDREN are not admiffible into the public fchools at Bofton, until feven years old: and they are there educated, the girls until they be twelve, and the boys until they arrive at the age of fourteen. At which time, the poor boys are fufficiently acquainted with the neceffary parts of education, to be put out to fome trade; while the girls, can follow purfuits becoming their different ftations in life.

N O T E.
* Dulce, et decorum eft, pro patria mori. HOR.

The schools for the girls, are entirely under the directions of masters; and if I be not mistaken, under those who have graduated at some college. They are here by just degrees instructed in all the solid parts of an American education, becoming their sex. I heard the dialogue between Syphax and Juba in the tragedy of Cato, read by several of them in the different schools; with a propriety and elegance commanding my greatest admiration. Poetry and prose, equally call their attention. Whether to follow Pope in his moral essays on man, or to converse with each other, in the instructive reading of dialogues, they exhibited a proficiency, which in girls between seven and twelve years of age was surprising. Writing and arithmetic, claim also a portion of their time. And a knowledge of grammar, early impressed upon their minds, directs them to a proper use of their own language.

The boys were examined in grammar, arithmetic, and geography; much to their honor and my gratification. They are instructed in an accurate knowledge of their own country, as well as in the grand outlines of the United States: and I believe are made acquainted with navigation, and furveying. They excell in beautiful writing. I have fome pieces of their performance in that way, which were prefented to me; and I hope they will be grateful to you at my return. When any boy difcovers a brightnefs of abilities, and defire of literary knowledge, he is removed to the Latin and Greek fchool: from whence, if he continue to merit the good opinion of his parents, he at a proper time is advanced to Cambridge college. There, to receive an education, ftill at the public expence, as far as relates to tuition. Thus we find, that the paths of knowledge are equally open here to the poor, as well as to the rich. Merit, like a beautiful flower, claims attention wherever found; is led through all the mazes of early life, to burft forth in full bloom, and to fpread its beauties upon the great carpet of nature.

ONE part of the neceffary education which the children receive, is in the particular care paid

paid to the pronunciation of their language. That the schools in America generally teach the pronunciation, is true; but I have never known any to expose the faults of pronunciation, in so forcible a manner as those, which are the subject of the present letter. The masters have for this purpose, selected, by way of illustration, a number of words generally miscalled: with which the children are instructed to be well acquainted. They are examined upon them, from time to time, and are taught to pronounce the word first in its proper way, and then to contrast it with the mode in which it is miscalled. As for example,

Boil,	is called	Boil,	and not	*Bile.*
Could,		Cou'd,		*Could.*
Cucumber,		Cucumber,		*Cowcumber.*
Certain,		Certain,		*Sartin.*
Merchant,		Merchant,		*Marchant.*
Molasses,		Molasses,		*Lasses.*
Onions,		Onions,		*Inions.*
Oil,		Oil,		*Ile.*
Point,		Point,		*Pint.*
Steady,		Steady,		*Study.*

It is by such means as these, which although simple

simple in themselves, yet by the forcible light in which the underſtanding is thereby ſtruck, fires in the memory of youth a juſt pronunciation of their language: which, in all probability will ever afterwards attend them through life. We ſhould not only be acquainted with the, ſmooth ſeas, but ſhould know where Scylla and Charybdis lie, that we may avoid them. For depend upon this truth, that although it be a good thing to know the proprieties of life, yet, it is alſo uſeful to be ſo much acquainted with the improprieties of that ſtation, as to enable us by a juſt contraſt, and firm conviction, to embrace the one, while we reject the other.

From the examination of the Engliſh ſchools we paſſed to that of the Latin, and Greek; conſiſting of about fifty ſcholars. Before the examination began, a ſalutatory oration in Latin, was delivered by a young gentleman of the ſenior claſs. After which, an examination took place, upon the Latin and Greek grammars, Clarke's introduction, Virgil, Horace and Homer. Then, a dialogue in Latin, was delivered

vered by the fenior clafs. After which a valedictory oration in Englifh was pronounced by one of that clafs, who bids fair to rife in literature. He is the fon of a blackfmith, educated at the public expence: and defervedly rifing, from meriting the favor of his countrymen*. May he continue to do fo. And never abufe the confidence of his fellow citizens, which from time to time he may enjoy.

The number of children which we faw at the different fchools, inclufively amounted to eleven hundred. I am informed, that there are about fourteen hundred educated at the public expence in this place. Many of them are children of genteel families; but by far the greater part, are poor children.

The examination at every fchool, ended with an *exhortation*, and a prayer; delivered by two gentlemen

N O T E.
* I underftood that in confideration of his talents, the felect-men had prefented him with a fmall annuity; to continue during his collegiate term of education.

gentlemen of the clergy succeſſively. How great an influence theſe had upon the hearers, is not for me to ſay. But for myſelf, I enjoyed a pleaſure of devotion and patriotiſm, which cannot be deſcribed. Sweet aſſemblage of two of the greateſt bleſſings to man, when rightly enjoyed! But when abuſed, the greateſt curſe which can befall him.

How often, have thoſe ſprings of action, miſuſed, ſwept, as with a broom of deſtruction, nations from the face of the earth? At this moment, Europe is ſhaken, and deluged with blood flowing from the oppoſition of paſſions unreſtrained, and pointed with all the ſeverity of malice, and revenge. Devoted to this frightful amalgam, ſee how St. Domingo is torn with every ſcourge of war. Peace, has long fled from it: Agriculture and commerce, are crippled to an extreme. Social liberty, although the cauſe of her misfortunes can ſcarcely find a reſting place for her feet upon that once happy, but now miſerable iſland. While at one ſtroke, her capital is burnt: and hundreds

dreds of her inhabitants sent bleeding into e-
ternity——Well, may the philanthropist weep
over this tragic scene: pointed, by the civil
commissioners Polverel, and Santhonax*. They
survive in the town: the first among *slaves;*
rather than to be on a footing *with the freemen,
who alone had a right to send them there.* But
peace, plenty, and happiness, crown our land,
thanks to propitious Heaven. Long, long,
may her sons, just to their own, and others
rights, deserve and enjoy this blessing. And
when the virtuous and the unfortunate, are
driven from all other parts of the world; here,
let them find rest to their wearied limbs, and
comfort, to their bleeding hearts.

Excuse this digression. An association of
ideas, request sometimes an indulgence from a
friend; however foreign they may immediately
be, from the subject considered. But, to return to that of education. And in doing so, I
will

N O T E.
* See their proclamation of the 21st June, 1793, da-
ted Cape-Francois.

will obferve, that public ones, are not confined to the town of Bofton alone; they are extended throughout the commonwealth of Maffachufetts. Equally careful of the morals, as well as of the education of youth; religion and tuition, go hand in hand throughout its extent. The commonwealth is divided into townfhips, which are fimilar to our parifhes, and counties; and each townfhip confifting of fifty houfe holders or upwards, is obliged to have and fupport a minifter of the proteftant religion, and a fchool mafter. And when they have one hundred families or houfe holders, they are obliged to have a grammar fchool for the acquifition of the languages: under a penalty recoverable at the court of quarter feffions, in cafe of default*.

The

N O T E.

* *The law refpecting this fubject, may be worth the reader's confideration; it is as follows:*

Laws of Maffachufett's Bay. 4th year of William and Mary. Chap. X. page 17.

An Act, for the fettlement and fupport of minifters and fchoolmafters.

BE it ordained, &c. that the inhabitants of each town within this province fhall take due care from time to time,

The consequence is, that although in this country every body be not learned; yet nobody is ignorant, and few are idle. They are trained to

NOTE—CONTINUED.

to be constantly provided of an able, learned, orthodox minister, or ministers, of good conversation, to dispense the word of God to them: which minister or ministers shall be suitably encouraged, and sufficiently supported and maintained by the inhabitants of such town. And all contracts agreements, and orders heretofore made, or that shall hereafter be made by the inhabitants of any town within this province, respecting their ministers or school masters, as to their settlement, or maintenance, shall remain good and valid, according to the true intent thereof, the whole time for which they were or shall be made in all the particulars thereof: and shall accordingly be pursued, put in execution and fulfilled. And when there is no contract and agreement, made in any town respecting the support and maintenance of the ministry: or when the same happens to be expired, and the inhabitants of such town shall neglect to make suitable provision therein: upon complaint thereof made unto the quarter sessions of the peace for the county where such town lies, the said court of quarter sessions shall and hereby are empowered to order a competent allowance unto such minister, according to the state and ability of such town: The same to be assessed upon the inhabitants by warrant from the court directed to the selectmen,

to habits of industry; and even make leisure subservient to good purposes. On Sundays, which are days of rest and refreshment, when passing

NOTE—CONTINUED.

who are thereupon to proceed to make and proportion such assessment in manner as directed for other public charges; and to cause the same to be levied by the constables of each town by warrant under the hands of the select-men; or of the town clerk, by their order.

Be it further, &c. That where any town shall be destitute of a minister qualified as aforesaid, and shall so continue by the space of six months, not having taken due care for the procuring, settling, and encouragement of such minister, the same being made to appear upon complaint unto their majesties' justices at the general sessions of the peace for the county: the said court of quarter sessions shall and hereby are empowered to make, an order upon every such defective town, speedily to provide themselves of such ministers as aforesaid, by the next sessions at the farthest. And in case such order be not complied with, then the said court shall take effectual care to procure a minister qualified as aforesaid, and order the charge of such minister's maintenance to be levied on the inhabitants of the town.

And it is further, &c. That the respective churches in the several towns within this province, shall at all times hereafter, use, exercise, and enjoy all their privileges and freedoms respecting divine service, church order, and discipline. And shall be encouraged in the peaceable and regular profession and practice thereof.

passing by the farmers' houses, I found many of them reading: and upon enquiry was told, that

NOTE—CONCLUDED.

And be it further, &c. That every town within this province having the number of fifty house-holders or upwards, shall be constantly provided of a school master to teach children and youth, to read and write. And where any town or towns have the number of one hundred families or householders, there shall also be a grammar school set up in every such town; and some discreet person of good conversation, well instructed in the tongues procured to keep such school. Every such school-master to be suitably encouraged, and paid by the inhabitants.

And the select men, and the inhabitants of such town respectively, shall take effectual care, to make due provision for the settlement and maintenance of such school-master and masters.

And if any town, qualified as before expressed, shall neglect the due observance of this act, for the procuring and settling of any such school-master as aforesaid, by the space of one year: every such defective town shall incur the penalty of ten pounds, for every conviction of such neglect: upon complaint made to their majesties' justices in quarter sessions, for the same county in which such defective town lieth; which penalty shall be towards the support of such school or schools within the same county, where there may be most need, at the discretion of the justices in quarter sessions: to be levied by warrant from the said court of sessions, in proportion, upon the inhabitants of such defective town, as other public charges and to be paid unto the county treasurer.

that they generally devote thofe days to reading religious books, the public laws, and the newfpapers*. Do you think it an eafy matter to enflave fuch a people? or to abufe public trufts with impunity? Whoever does, muft be as much mifled, as were the Britifh miniftry; who under God's bleffing, were the mean of breaking our fubjection to Great-Britain.

WITH fuch inhabitants, a country is really ftrong. Taught to know their own rights, they are indignant of injury: and are ever on the watch, to detect mal-adminiftration in government. Property, reputation, and life, are fafe in a country like this: for none but well informed juries can give judgment refpecting them. Not fuch as you, and I, have feen—None of whom could write; and the foreman barely able to fet his mark to a *general verdict*. I blufh, for the fituation of *thofe*, which has enabled

N O T E.

* IT is fuppofed that at leaft thirty thoufand Newfpapers are circulated each week throughout the New-England ftates. MORSE.

enabled me to say this. But it is too true. And that it may speedily change for the better; that *they* may become more industrious, and better informed; that both religion and education may walk the round in Carolina, producing as happy effects as they have done in Massachusetts; is the sincere wish of your affectionate friend.

LETTER VII.

Arrival at Portsmouth, in the State of New-Hampshire. A description of the town. Recommended as an agreeable abode, during the summer months. A fowling and fishing party. A conversation respecting the connexion between the Southern and Eastern States. Mention made of Dartmouth College, and a linen and cambrick manufactory. A similar one recommended to be established at Winnsborough in the State of South-Carolina. Account of the road between Boston and Portsmouth: leading to a description of a bridge over the Merrimack River.

Portsmouth, July 29, 1793.

I HAVE been here since last Monday, and shall return to-morrow to Boston. What a contrast do I experience in being at the latter place, and at this. There, a continued clatter is kept up throughout the day, by carriages rolling upon the paved streets: here, a calm, and quiet reigns, inviting one to every mental gratification.

gratification. At this moment, while I am writing, do I enjoy the music of two hemp birds: undisturbed by a noisy town. At one time, they seem to hold converse with each other; at another time, they seem to strive which can sing loudest, and with the greatest variety of notes. How much like two friends travelling together in the path of human life. Alternately, enjoying the sweets of friendship; or, following the impulse of a well directed ambition.

This, though a small town, contains about five thousand inhabitants. Its streets are not paved, except occasionally on the sides. Its harbour, is one of the best in the United States: for although not large, yet it can boast of a great depth of water. Ships of any burden, may lie at its wharves, protected from wind by the best land-locked harbour, which I have seen. The town is retired about a league from the sea, and is situated upon Piscataqua River; which may be more than a quarter of a mile wide. And from its occasional windings among the

the heights, and the extreme force of the tide, running at the rate of seven knots an hour, and forming very strong eddies, becomes extremely difficult of accefs to a belligerent fleet. In so much, that although many of the British ships during the American war were occafionally at the mouth of the river; yet, none of them dared attempt the paffage to the town. The tide here rises about fifteen feet, which is the cause of the great velocity with which it runs. And its quicknefs, why it is never frozen up in winter: which gives an evident advantage over some ports in the northern and eaftern ftates of America.

The harbour, is quite deftitute of fhipping at prefent; there being not more, than three or four fail in it. All their veffels and failors being engaged at this time either on freight, or in the fifhing trade. Thirty fail have been invited from hence fouthwardly, by the high freights given in confequence of the prefent European war. And this vaft demand which is at prefent for fhipping, is one reafon, why

there

there reigns here, fo great a calm; and why fuch a vaſt number of women are feen, entirely difproportionate to the men.

At this place during our ſtruggle for independence, a feventy-four gun ſhip called ' *The America,*' was built; and prefented by Congrefs to the king of France. She is now in the French navy: and has been lately in active fervice in the Weſt-Indies. For the building of this ſhip, the public were indebted to the fpirited exertions of Mr. John Langdon*; whofe unceafing perfeverance overcame difficulties, which entirely fruſtrated the attempts of others, in fimilar cafes.

Here, bleffed with a fine fummer climate, one may enjoy a focial retirement; very fimilar to that of a country life. A genteel houfe,
with

N O T E.
* Now a fenator from the ſtate of N. Hampſhire, in the Congrefs of the United States.

with a garden, carriage houfe and appurtenances may be had at the rate of thirty pounds sterling per annum. A large frefh cod-fifh capable of dining four or five perfons, may be bought for as many coppers. A fat turkey for a quarter dollar, and meats upon as cheap a fcale. Indeed, I have never met with a place, where fo many circumftances combined to form an agreeable retreat. Should fifhing, or fowling fometimes be an object of recreation, by going to the mouth of the river, one is furnifhed with both. The other day, I went down to an ifland with a fowling party; and by juft ftanding upon one fpot, and fhooting at pidgeons as they flew over our heads, we killed many dozen. Sometimes, I would defcend from the hill upon which I was placed, into the valley; in order to fee fome men catch pidgeons with a fpring net. This is very amufing; and equally fuccefsful. I will endeavor to defcribe to you the manner, by which they are taken.

Two or three men, after having provided themfelves with a proper net, two or three flutter pidgeons, and one or two fliers, arrive at the proper ground before day: where, they prepare for action. For this purpose, they firſt erect a ſmall ſkreen of buſhes in a circular form. Then, they ſet the net: which by lines communicates to the ſkreen. They then place under the ſweep of the net, but upon the ground, the flutter pidgeons; (ſo called from being fixed to a flutter ſtick, which by reaſon of a ſtring communicating to the ſkreen, they raiſe up and down, when the pidgeons are flying over) and have the flier pidgeon ready on a rooſt, tied to the ſkreen by a long ſtring: the eyes of all theſe decoy pidgeons, being firſt ſewed up. As ſoon as the men perceive a flock of pidgeons coming over, they immediately throw up the flier: which flies to the extent of the ſtring, and then falls down. This, draws the attention of the pidgeons, and they immediately light within the ſweep of the net; enticed there, by the decoy flutter pidgeons. The ſpring line is then drawn; and they are covered with the net. And in this way, as many as thirty dozen have been caught at once.

AFTER

After amufing ourfelves in this manner from five to eight o'clock in the morning, we went a fifhing. And although our lines were in bad order, we in the courfe of an hour caught two fine codfifh, and between one and two hundred other fifh. When the Prefident of the United States was here, inftead of wedding the fea as the Doge of Venice does, he may be faid to have received a tribute from it; for, I am informed, he caught a codfifh himfelf, when indulging in one of thefe parties.

The connexion between the individual ftates of the union, formed the other day a fubject of converfation in a company, where I was prefent. Many, were the opinions delivered refpecting it: but none more worthy of remark than what an efteemed political character, whofe acquaintance I have the honor to enjoy, faid upon that occafion. " I told my friends
' B——r, and I——d, what they would not
' then, but now begin to believe; that the fouth-
' ern ftates were clofely connected in interefts
' with the eaftern. The one has a great deal of
' fhipping;

' shipping; the other, a quantity of produce.
' Hence, they are mutually dependent; the one,
' for ships: and the other, for freight. Parti-
' cularly at this time, when, owing to the pre-
' sent European war, American vessels enjoy
' much of the carrying trade. We are in a si-
' tuation, which enables us to build ships cheap-
' er, than can be done in the southern states.
' And is it then an object of no importance to
' be on a friendly footing with a country capa-
' ble of supplying a want of vessels, at a short
' notice, and upon reasonable terms? Is it an ob-
' ject of no importance, to be careless about
' the produce of a country, which gives life
' and spirit to navigation? Or, can the interests
' of the southern states in that particular suffer;
' without materially injuring those of the east-
' ern?"——He spoke truth. Try the probable
actions of men in all ages, by this test; and
one can draw a just conclusion.

They have schools in this state similar to
those in Massachusetts; and also a college*,

N O T E.
* Dartmouth College.

situated

situated on Connecticut river; at the extreme interior part of the state: which, is now rising into respectability.

At Londonderry, a town retired about forty miles from the sea, is a tolerably extensive linen and cambrick manufactory; where much of those stuffs are made: and of a tolerable fineness. For this, they are indebted to some Irish who settled it: and who, wherever they go, generally carry this useful knowledge with them. Why, cannot we have such a manufactory at Winnsborough? Its lands are suited to the culture of flax; and its country peopled by a vast number of Irish inhabitants. Let but some person of enterprise and fortune, assist the attempt; and I am deceived, if the farmers thereabouts, will not find it more to their advantage, than their present pursuits in agriculture. By this mean, their strength will be called forth: and even their children when a little advanced in years, will afford them an astonishing assistance. While, exclusive of the flax for the manufactory, their annual income in money,

will

will be encreafed by the fale of the feed. Need I fay that the community at large, would be thereby benefited? No one who has ever indulged a thought refpecting exportation, and manufactures, can do otherwife than approve the encreafing of both the one, and the other.

THE whole way from Bofton to Portfmouth, is a thickly populated, and well cultivated country: the road is perhaps one of the fineft in the United States. You pafs from farm to farm, from village to village, and from town to town, in quick fucceffion. Some few miles from Bofton is a fmall village called Lynn; celebrated for the vaft quantities of fhoes made there for exportation. The fhoe-makers fhops, are almoft equal to the number of dwelling houfes in the town. The road leads through the town of Salem, Beverly, and Newbury-port: which, for riches and commerce, have a right to be confidered as fome of the moft refpectable towns in America.

TWO or three miles beyond Newbury-port,

is

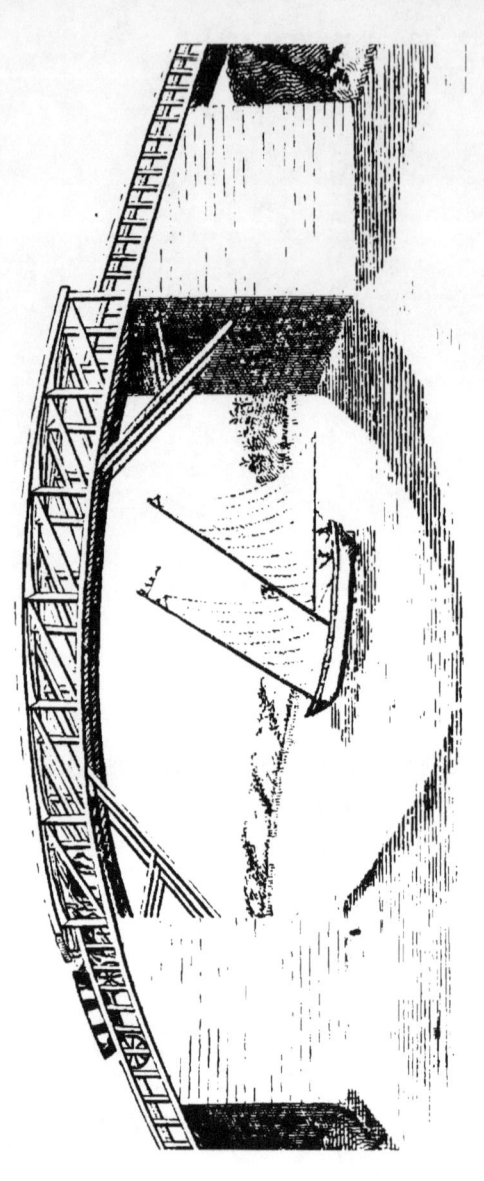

is a beautiful wooden bridge of one arch, thrown acrofs the Merrimack river: whofe length, is one hundred and fixty feet; and whofe height, is forty feet above the level of high water. For beauty and ftrength, it has certainly no equal in America: and I doubt whether as a wooden bridge, there be any to compare with it elfewhere. The ftrength of the bridge is much encreafed above the common mode in ufe, by pieces of timber placed upon it, and fhouldered into each other. They run upon the bridge, in three lines; parrallel with the length of the bridge, and with each other; fo as to make two diftinct paffage-ways for carriages. Thefe braces, are fome feet in height, and are connected on the top by crofs pieces. affording fufficient room for carriages to pafs underneath, without inconvenience. It is faid, that the upper work has as great a tendency to fupport the weight of the bridge; as the fleepers, upon which it is built. I had not time to ftay there longer than five minutes; fo muft be excufed in a fketch which I have taken of it: and that was not done upon the fpot, but only by recollection. If in fo doing, I fhould perfuade others to en-

quire.

quire more particularly refpecting it; and to adopt what may be good in its mechanifm; my object will be gratified. The river, over which it is built, is fubject to frefhes: it is therefore high from the general current of the water: and as being proper for that, I apprehend would not be unfuitable to fimilar rivers in Carolina.

LETTER

LETTER VIII.

Account of the Humane Society at Boston, for the relief of ship-wrecked persons. The Society visit the huts upon the islands. Character of the clergy. A description of Castle-William. Convicts sent there, to labor: not benefiting their morals. Description of Boston. Taxes. Hackney coaches. Trades and manufactures. The Mall. The Column. The town of Cambridge, and Harvard College. The two bridges over Charles-River.

Boston, August 4, 1793.

I DOUBT whether there be any country, where the wants of the unfortunate are more respected, than in the commonwealth of Massachusetts. Her fostering hand leads the youth into life; and is afterwards ready to be extended, when any unfortunate emergency may offer. Of their institutions for the relief of misfortune, there is none which affords me more satisfaction than one for the assistance of ship-wrecked people;

ple; called the Humane Society. It is formed by some of the most respectable men of the town, as well clergy, as laity. From whose fund, small huts are built upon the islands most exposed to ship-wreck, for the relief of those, whose good fortune may bring them to land, escaped from the dangers of the sea.

These huts, are generally placed upon uninhabited islands: and are furnished with blankets, wood, tinder-box, candles, salt provisions, biscuit, and such other things, which although not the luxuries, are yet the necessaries of life. They are visited once every year, by the society, and such gentlemen as they may choose to invite: for the purpose of seeing whether the hut, and necessaries placed in them, are in good order. It was my good fortune to be of the party, which went down the harbour upon that occasion. We were in number about forty; and sailed in a packet, attended by a handsome twelve oared barge. Such is the respect paid to this society by the government, that upon these occasions it is always honored

by

by a federal falute of cannon, from the caftle; as well when going, as when returning. This we had the pleafure of receiving; in addition to the fweet approbation of an honeft heart, and well directed purfuit. And believe me, when I confider it as one of the moft rational days, paffed fince I left you. I am informed that thefe huts have already been the means of faving to the commonwealth, the lives of many of its citizens: while the fociety judicioufly diftributes rewards to thofe, whofe exertions have ferved the diftreffed.

It was upon this occafion, that I became acquainted with fome of the moft refpectable clergymen of the town. Men, whofe liberality of fentiment, and refpectability of manners won my efteem. I have ever drawn near when opportunities allowed, to men of erudition; and particularly to thofe cloathed in the garment of religion. And when I found them pleafed to difcourfe upon fubjects which might afford me information, I loft not the opportunity of attending to them. It was my happinefs to be

thus

thus fituated. Inftead of exhibiting countenances, which feemed to frown over the vanities, and even amufements of life; and to defpife every thing, which wore not the forbidding and felf-denying afpect of puritanical religion; they appeared gentle in manners, and focial in company: without defcending from that dignity of deportment, in which their calling directs them to move. It is with fuch monitors, fuch companions as thefe, that I would gather the flowers of religion: and that I would pafs through the meads of life, with grateful thanks to a bountiful God. While the fanatic fhall weep through the misfortunes of life, let me, confcious that the fmiles of creation are more acceptable to heaven than its tears, offer up my thanks with a grateful, but not the lefs fmiling adoration. Satisfied, that as the fields enameled with flowers, afford more pleafure, than when they are covered with fnow; fo a cheerful, and contented mind, is beft fuited for the thanks, which either the illiterate or learned can pay.

I DID not omit paying a vifit to Caftle-William. It is fituated in the harbour of Bofton, a league a league below the town: upon an island containing about thirty acres of land. There is a beautiful archipelago of islands in this harbour, in number, amounting to about forty: all of which, have high grounds upon them. Upon the height of one of these islands, the castle is placed. In some parts of it, there is a stone foundation; but in others, the height of the land is only assisted with ramparts, and merlons of turf. I am informed it was formerly furnished with three tier of cannon. The first consisting of heavy ones, placed at the waters edge: and the other two upon platforms at the embrasures. But now, they are placed upon the middle battery, except thirteen small ones, which being round the flag-staff en barbette, serve for the purpose of saluting. The castle is very much out of order at present; the platforms and carriages for guns, being much injured by the weather. However, even in its present situation it is very respectable: and is well provided with mortars, cannon, bombs, ball, and double-headed shot. From its near situation to the channel, its guns can shoot with much effect, upon vessels passing to, or from the

the town. Here, I faw an eighteen pounder, which the Britifh had difabled of its trunnions, re-mounted and fit for fervice, upon a carriage, invented for that particular purpofe. It is made of white oak, and is faid to anfwer very well.

There are now within the caftle, barracks edual to the lodgement of a thoufand men: befides many buildings upon the ifland, without its gates. The ground within the earth, is interfected at proper diftances by covered ways: and the magazine is protected from accidents. Here, are now mounted about thirty pieces of heavy cannon, befides fome fmaller ones. It is garrifoned by a company of infantry upon pay, at the expence of the commonwealth: who alfo guard the convicts here fent, convicted of crimes deferving punifhment lefs than death. They are condemned to labour for a certain term of years, or for life: of whom, feventy are now on the ifland, chiefly employed in the nail manufactory.

I went into the blackfmiths fhop, which is a long

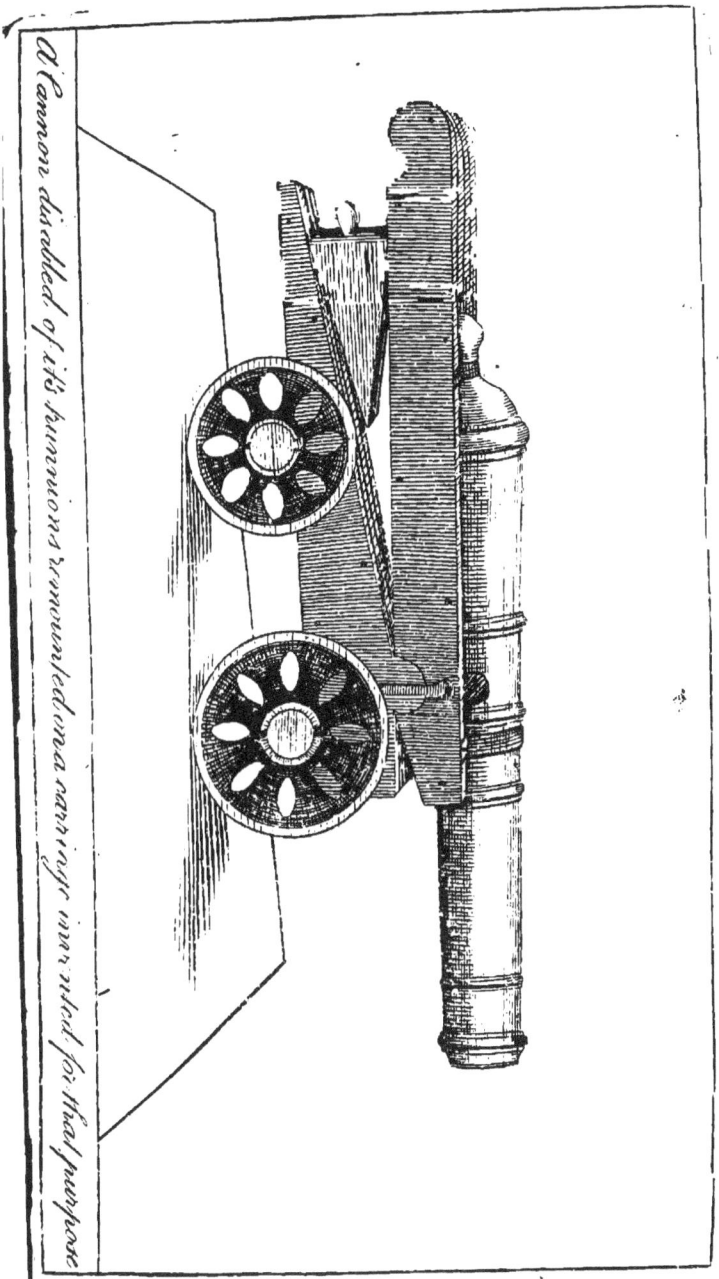

A cannon disabled of it's ammunition & mounted on a carriage unsuited for that purpose

long building, with several forges in it; but, I assure you I was soon glad to leave it: for never was I atracked by such a set of importunate sturdy beggars in my life. I had no opportunity of making any observations, or asking any questions; so incessantly did their shamelefs demands wring in mine ears. I hastened from a place, where I saw there was nothing to be gained; and much, to be loft. For, although it be a pleasure to me in reflecting, that I have never in my life withholden assistance from the unfortunate; yet it is also my satisfaction to avoid throwing it away upon the undeserving. In the midst of such a confusion of tongues, of entreaties, and of oaths; it was impossible to make any discrimination. While some were begging, others, were as earnest, that nothing should be given them: charging them with being unworthy of charity—Disgusted at the scene, I left them to the punishment which their crimes had deservedly brought down, upon their heads.

This, is the effect of the humane laws of this country; punishing few crimes with death.

One

One would imagine that Mr. Howard's plan of punishment, were the original, from whence they were copied; so much, do they coincide with it. "I would wish (says he) that no per-
" sons might suffer capitally, but for *murder*,
" for *setting houses on fire*, for *house breaking*,
" *attended with acts of cruelty*. The highway-
" man—the foot-pad—the habitual thief, and
" people of this clan: should end their days in
" a penetentiary house, rather than on the
" gallows." *

The manner in which the convicts are kept at the castle, may be politically right: but, it certainly is morally wrong. For placed in this public manner to an ignominious slavery, under no controul but that necessary for their immediate safety; they become callous to every principle of shame: while their greatest pleasure is to boast of the feats they have performed;

claiming

N O T E.
Howard's State of Prisons, p. 42.

claiming pre-eminence among their fellow sufferers in proportion to the rascality of their former lives.. I know a gentleman of this town, whose house was robbed at mid-day of seventy guineas, by one of these fellows: and being some time afterwards at the castle he was accosted by the fellow, and asked, " Whether he had " ever known who had stolen the money?" Upon the gentleman's answering in the negative, he said " He had done it :" and then related with much satisfaction the manner in which he had performed so gallant an action. Can these men, ever be of service to society again? Can principles of honor, shame or fear, ever restrain within proper bounds their licentious actions? Reason, seems to revolt at the idea. They are published to the world as villains, know themselves as such: and are even ambitious of deserving the character.

THEY cannot then be placed here to benefit their morals, and recall them back to a virtuous life: for it is evident, their situation has a contrary tendency. The old, here glory in their
villainy;

villainy; and the young, in being mixed with them, are only sent to be instructed in vice. It must therefore be justified upon policy; and that can only properly relate to those, who are condemned to be there for life. They must be considered as having forfeited all claims of protection from society; which, should be screened from their further depredations. Not, by inflicting death: for as I have said before, their laws do not require it. But by confining them from opportunities of doing farther mischief; and making that confinement beneficial to the community, which, they have injured.

A STRANGER at Boston, soon remarks the industry of its inhabitants; and their attention to business. While, he laments that so noted a town in the page of history, were not regulated by a better police. It is under the controul of select-men, as indeed all the other towns of the commonwealth are: but their powers, are too much abridged by reason of their town meetings, to undertake any thing
of

of efficiency, without having recourse to the opinions of a multifarious assembly. Few lamps assist the passenger through the streets by night, and if ever they were necessary in any place, they certainly are in this. For the streets are crooked, and narrow; paved from side to side with round stones, extremely disagreeable, and inconvenient to those who walk them: and for this reason, strangers are more apt to ride about this, than any other town on the continent. In many streets there are no railings or posts, to defend one from the carriages, which are incessantly traversing them. Carts, waggons, drays, trucks, wheel-barrows, and porters, are continually obstructing the passage in these streets: While, the people concerned in this kind of business, are not apt to put themselves out of the way, for the pleasure of conferring favors. They seem so conscious that all men are equal, that they take a pride in shewing their knowledge of this principle upon every occasion, *without adverting to its use.* I have seen a porter with a little hand cart pursuing his destination in the street, with the utmost unconcern; at the risk of being crippled, or having his cart crushed

crushed to pieces by a carriage which was thundering in his ears. And having escaped misfortune, he reviled the coachman, and asked him if he did not see him? The same question might have been retorted in answer, with the addition of 'did not you hear me?' Nothing, but the most sullen and unaccommodating disposition, could have hindered him from giving way to a carriage; which could turn aside less easily, than he might have done.

There cannot be a greater nuisance in any town, and particularly in this, than the allowance of hucksters, to occupy part of the streets, during the day. Either the overseers of the markets and streets, are not invested with sufficient powers to remedy the evil; or some reason, of which, I am uninformed, forbids their putting them in force. One would imagine, that with such heavy taxes as the Bostonians labour under, much more, might be done for their convenience. It may truly be said, that they are taxed, not by what they are worth: but by what their appearances in life are.

Hence,

Hence, the reafon, why fome monied men among them, make no fhow; and are without noife continually amaffing wealth, and confining it within their immediate grafp, to the difadvantage of the fociety at large. While others of more generous difpofitions, are called upon to pay a much larger tax, than they fhould in juftice do. The taxes are impofed by affeffors upon their eftate, ftock in trade, and in the funds : and unlefs the citizens prove to their fatisfaction, that they do not poffefs a fortune equal to their affeffment, they are obliged to pay the tax. This publication they are unwilling to make, particularly mercantile men : who deem it improper that perfons might thus be informed of their private circumftances. Hence, fome refpectable and rich citizens have left the town : an example, which may be followed by others, fhould this fyftem of taxation not be altered.

No place in America is perhaps equal to Bofton, for excellent hackney coaches. From nine o'clock in the morning, to the fame hour in the evening,

evening, they are on the stand in State-street; and are ready at a moment's warning.

ALL kinds of trades, flourish in this industrious place. Among their manufactures, there are none more worthy of being noticed, than that of glass, wool-cards, sail-duck, and fishing-hooks. The machines for the making of the wool-cards, is extremely ingenious: and said to be invented by an inhabitant of the town. It is supposed to be superior to any thing of the kind in Europe. Every piece of the wooden work, is fashioned out by a particular machine; so that the utmost uniformity is observable among the different parts of the wooden work. The wires, are cut and bent, at the same time; which is considered as a great and expeditious improvement. The duck manufactory carries on a vast deal of business; and supplies much of the shipping with sails. It employs three hundred and sixty persons; seventy of whom are girls: and works twenty-seven looms. The importation of sail cloth has been greatly reduced, since this manufacture

ture has been eftablifhed ; in fo much, that a gentleman who had been in the habit of annually importing four thoufand pieces of fail cloth from Ruffia, informed me, he now only imports two thoufand, from that place.

EXCLUSIVE of the pleafure arifing, from feeing the profperity of individuals, a fatisfaction is enjoyed, when viewing thefe public benefits. They, fhould ever be encouraged by the public favor, as being intimately connected with a country's independence. It is time, that we fhould begin to throw off the fhackles, of a too long monopolized commerce. The United States, within their embrace hold every thing, which the neceffaries of mankind, or even fome of their luxuries demand. They only wait to be brought forth, by proper means. It is their policy, to encreafe the articles of exportation; and to reduce thofe of importation. Thus, the balance of trade will be in their favor ; and that not in goods, but in money.

It is not the statesman, who supinely passing life away, and barely leading forth adventitious sources of aggrandizement to a state, that deserves its praise. It is he, whose daring and penetrating spirit, o'erleaps the bounds of opposition: that merits the plaudits of his countrymen. It is to the exertions of such men, that countries may arise to that knowledge, strength, and importance in a short time; which, in the common course of things, must wait for the return of centuries to obtain. Happy for America, should such men come forward in her service. Still happier, should party spirit, or low minded jealousy, not check or embarrass their patriotic exertions.

There is a public walk in Boston, called the mall: which is very agreeable. It is upwards of half a mile long, and offers to your choice both a gravel, and a turf walk; shaded by beautiful elm trees. A street runs parallel with it on one side; and on the other a large common: where hundreds of cattle feed during the day. This common on the further side, rises

rises up to a confiderable height. At one end of the walk is a profpect of a large bafon of water, Roxbury town, and Charles river: at the other, the town of Bofton, and column upon Beacon hill.

THIS column has been lately erected, in commemoration of remarkable events which took place, during the American war: and in honor of its prefent efficient government. It is about fixty feet high: crowned on the top with a golden eagle ftanding upon a globe, and overlooking the arms of the United States. This fpot, is the higheft elevation about Bofton. From it, may be feen over the tops of all the houfes, the iflands in the harbour, the light houfe, many leagues at fea, and a vaft diftance into the country. Bunker's hill, here heaves into view. It was there, that Americans perceived their own ftrength; and that Britifh hirelings expofed their own weaknefs. It is now, in fields of agriculture. How different to what it was, when meffengers of death, were hurled over its land! Well, are Americans admonifhed

monifhed from an infcription on the bafe of the column; that while the profpects of agriculture and commerce prefent themfelves to the fight, where, war was accuftomed to found the difcordant clarion; they fhould not be forgetful of thofe, who were affifting to their now happy fituation. Who, taught them their rights; and learned them, how they were to be defended.

From hence, is feen the town of Cambridge, at three miles diftance. Celebrated as being the place, where General Wafhington took the command of the continental army *, and alfo for the inftitution of Harvard college: provided with the beft appointment of philofophical apparatus that I have met with. Among which is a complete and elegant orrery, conftructed by Mr. Pope; without his ever having feen one. The college, is furnifhed with a library of

N O T E.

* Ramfay's Ame. Rev. Vol. I. p. 220.

of fourteen thousand volumes, selected with learning and taste: and affording an ample fund both of antient, and modern information.

Here, if a young man will but pursue the intent of his destination; much knowledge may be acquired in the course of three or four years. The college being under the direction of a president and professors of learning and integrity, leads him to every avenue of improvement; while the expence which is not more than two hundred pounds sterling, throws in his way, no unnecessary obstacle. The number of students at this college are from one hundred and fifty to two hundred. On the second Wednesday in July, they receive degrees. This day, is the most brilliant in the calendar of the commonwealth; being made so, by the policy of government for the encouragement of education. The public officers, the civil, the military, and the religious, all join upon this great occasion to form a procession in honor of the day. I was at the commencement, and assisted sincerely ly in offering up my beſt wiſhes for the proſperity of the inſtitution: for the advancement of learning and morality within its walls, and the extenſion of its fame, through all the country round.

From this hill, alſo is ſeen the bridge over Charles river, connecting Boſton with Charleſtown: and another partly finiſhed, opening a more eaſy communication with Cambridge. The firſt is about a quarter of a mile long; the latter will be more than twice its length. They have each of them ſide ways, for foot paſſengers. are illuminated at night by lamps, and are built of wood: which, in all probability, will laſt long without repair; as the worm does not bite in theſe northern latitudes. Would to Heaven that we were not viſited by theſe plagues, to every nautical enterprize. But why ſhould I repine? Is not nature laviſh with her bounties? Though ſhe does not ſtrew all her different kinds of flowers over every part of the globe, yet there is ſcarcely the clime, where a bouquet

may

may not be made up for the object of one's affections; or where, happiness may not be obtained, when mankind are directed by industry and prudence.

The shuddering tenant of the frigid zone
Boldly proclaims that happiest spot his own,
Extols the treasures of his stormy seas,
And his long night of revelry and ease;
The naked savage, panting at the line,
Boasts of his golden sands, and palmy wine,
Basks in the glare, or stems the tepid wave,
And thanks his Gods, for all the good they gave.
Nor less the patriot's boast where'er we roam,
His first, best country, ever is, at home.

And yet perhaps, if countries we compare,
And estimate the blessings which they share;
Though patriots flatter, still shall wisdom find
An equal portion dealt to all mankind;
As different good, by art or nature given
To different nations, makes their blessings even.
   GOLDSMITH'S TRAVELLER.

LETTER

LETTER IX.

Journey from Boston, to New-Haven. Description of Springfield: where the federal arsenal for the Eastern States is kept. Description of Hartford, and Middletown. Of Durham: a triste sejour on Sundays for travellers. Description of New-Haven; and state of Yale college. Manufactures. Divorces obtained in Connecticut. The opinion which a traveller is likely to form in passing through the Eastern States.

New-York, August 31, 1793.

I ARRIVED at this city on Thursday morning, having left Boston the Friday before. The greatest part of the way I came by land, in order to see a part of Connecticut state. Upon this route while travelling in the state of Massachusetts, we early the second morning, burst from an high sandy pine barren, upon the heights of Springfield. Here, the federal arsenal for the Eastern states is kept; consisting of
several

several thousand stand of arms, and other military stores. At the time of Shay's rebellion, his party endeavoured to obtain possession of it. But here, his imaginary laurels, withered on his brow; and himself and hopes sunk into the shade of oblivion. The town is situated about seventy miles westward of Boston, in a thickly populated country upon Connecticut river. The view from these heights is pleasing; particularly as coming so suddenly to the sight. From them, the traveller looks down upon the town at their feet: sees farms scattered every where round the country: overlooks the river, and ends his prospect with the distant heights.

IMMEDIATELY below this, we crossed the river; being there about three hundred yards wide. It is the prettiest one in the Eastern states; running through Connecticut and Massachusetts, and losing itself in the states of New-Hampshire and Vermont: traversing in its course, a vast extent of country. Down this river much of the exports of the upper states are

are carried to Connecticut: by which mean, her exports, are nominally greater, while those of Massachusetts and New-Hampshire are proportionably smaller. At the melting of the snows, the river comes down in all its majesty; rising about fifteen feet perpendicular: and overflowing the land on either side. The lands which are overflowed are called *intervale*, are used as meadows, and occasionally sown with hemp and grain. On each side of the river is a tolerable quantity of this land, extremely productive: and the up lands along the course of the river are also good, and of a clayey texture.

We passed through Hartford in the course of the day, it is situated on Connecticut river, is a town of much prosperity and affluence; and contains many genteel buildings. Towards the evening we came in sight of Middletown, situated upon the same river. And never was I more mortified, than in the knowledge that I had neither time or ability, to sketch so complicated

plicated a scene; description can never equal it. Not only, because it can never be perfect; but also, on account of the necessary length of a description of prospect; which, by reason of its tediousness can never bring the collected idea of perspective full to the imagination. All, that can be imagined of a country situation, may be conceived of this. We saw it, from an height at the distance of three miles, just at the bend of the river: which led down to it, in a straight direction, and with a gentle current. It was just at the time, when the setting sun gilds with delightful brightness the spiry steeples; when

" ———————————— it tips the mountains brow,
" The cottage roof, and glimmers o'er the vale;"

it was just at this time, that we saw it, contrasted with the beautiful shades of verdure, led on by the evening hours. The eye, with joy viewed the country round; and saw it rising in sweet luxuriance of autumnal dress, to a distance of many miles. Such, and much more, than I can describe, is the prospect about Middletown: which, not to have seen, would have been

been unpardonable in any perfon travelling through that country for pleafure, or information.

On Saturday night, we arrived at Durham, a fmall village in Connecticut ftate; and twenty miles from New-Haven. A trifle fejour on Sundays for travellers, whofe misfortune brings them there the evening before. Nothing could perfuade the driver to carry us on to New-Haven on Sunday. It feems this reluctance to travel on that day, is in obedience to a law of the ftate; impofing a penalty upon thofe who do. This, is the only mark of bigotry, which I have met with in the eaftern ftates: and that only in the ftate of Connecticut. I am informed that in fome parts of it, the law is not inforced: however, I was forry to find it would be enforced any where in the ftate, at this period of time. Liberality of fentiment is now fo general in religions, throughout America; that I flatter myfelf the legiflature of that ftate will foon repeal a law, which cafts no honor upon

the

the code of so respectable a community. At ten o'clock on Sunday, the landlord waited on my companion and myself, to ask us to meeting. You may imagine we did not accept his invitation. We were chagrined sufficiently, in thus being arrested on our journey; without still further subjecting ourselves to the mortification, of being publicly exposed to the view of a large congregation. However, to beguile the tedious hours, we requested some books; and he was condescending enough to favor us with some classical ones; (for it seems he was a scholar) among which, I was happy in finding an Horace: wherein, the *iter Brundusium*, and other pieces applicable to our then situation, in some measure made us amends for this encroachment on our liberty.

WE however arrived at New-Haven on Monday; from whence, I proposed to proceed to New-York by water. This town, and Hartford, are occasionally the seats of government of this state. It is situated at the head of a

bay,

bay, which opens into the found, running between Long-Ifland and the Main: and is an agreeable retreat, being quiet and airy. To Yale College in this town, many eminent characters in America owe their education. I am informed there are generally one hundred and fifty ftudents at it. Their library is but fmall, having only 2,700 volumes in it: and thofe, principally antient. While their philofophical apparatus is on a confined fcale, in contraft with thofe, of other American feminaries.

This town, is faid to have been the retreat of three of the regicides of Charles the firft— Their names were, lieutenant general Edward Whalley, major general William Goff, and colonel John Dixwell; who at the reftoration in the year 1660 fled to America, and were fecreted in Maffachufetts and Connecticut for near thirty years. They are faid to have lived a part of that time in a cave, at Weft Rock; four miles from the town. Dixwell's tomb ftone was fhewn me, which, if I be not miftaken,
mentions,

mentions him to be there buried in the year 1688: his name is not carved at length upon it, but only *J. D. Esquire*. It is much injured by the weather, and somewhat reduced in size by the attentions of English travellers and antiquaries, who break off pieces from it, to carry away with them. Mr. Styles, prefident of the college, has written their hiftory; which will no doubt when publifhed afford entertainment to the curious.

There are two metal button manufactories in this place; where, I saw them made with diligence, and difpatch; and by no means inferior to thofe of a fimilar kind imported from England.

In this ftate, divorces may be obtained. It has been the policy of fome countries, and of our own, not to allow them: as leading to a greater levity of conduct and unhappinefs in the married ftate, when they can thus eafely get
rid

rid of it; than when, although separated from each other, they are interdicted from forming new connexions. But nature, place, and circumstances, have different influences: and what may be allowable in one country, may be improper in another.

Throughout the New-England states, the traveller is pleased in observing the decent and respectful attention which he meets with from the youth of both sexes. Wherever he goes, he will not be disappointed in receiving their salutes. They are attentive in the observance of this etiquette: which they learn in their public schools never to omit. Nothing can be more pleasingly offered to the mind, as a mark of the civilization of a people, than this mode; of early instructing their little ones in due principles of subordination, and respect to their elders. It becomes a source of real happiness, in private families; and as they advance in years, tends to make them citizens obedient to the laws of their country. They have many things to make them so, and nothing more than the freedom and impartiality with which members for the different legiſlatures are elected. To canvaſs for votes, is effectually to cruſh the expectations of a candidate. Hence, men are elected whoſe characters lead them to the appointment; and who conſequently enjoy the confidence of the citizens. And for the ſame reaſon, it is rare to ſee young men filling public ſtations, or turning out tried ſervants of the public, by dint of electioneering influence. That, is only the caſe in countries; where, novelty enters deeply into the national character; or where, a long train of corruption in manners has firſt paved the way for it.

With the New-Englandmen, this is not to be found; for they may truly be ſaid to be independent both in circumſtances and principles. Independent, in circumſtances, as being always induſtrious; and not panting after unattainable enjoyments. In principles, as not being of deſperate fortunes, they are in the habit of enjoying

joying their own opinions, without subjecting themselves to the designs of others. Thus, preserving a steady course, as well in private as in public life, they possess a character jealous of liberty; and indignant of every attempt, which would seduce them from their own immediate interests: or make them swerve from that of their country's good. Hence, faction finds no resting place amongst them, to corrode with the sourness of her leaven, their domestic happiness. Chased away, by the knowledge of a well informed people; she flies to where, ignorance and idleness. mould the people for her views, and subject them to the destructive ravages of her empire.

LETTER

LETTER X.

Mobs at New-York. The cause of them, with considerations thereon. Sickness at Philadelphia.

New-York, October 16, 1793.

SINCE last Monday, this city has been disquieted at night by mobs; who, not content with patroling the streets, have been the cause of some mischief. The occasion of it, was this. During the last week a cause was tried, wherein a young man was indicted of a r—e; and was regularly acquitted. This gave great umbrage to a particular class of citizens; who were decidedly of opinion that he should have been hanged. They spoke warmly against him in different companies, and upon different occasions: until by such means encreasing the fermentation of their passions, they broke out into the extravagancies of a licentious mob.

THE

The firſt thing upon which this torrent burſt was Mrs. Carey's houſe: it was ſaid that ſhe had been his friend upon the occaſion, and that her houſe had been uſeful to him. They attacked it; and levelled it with the ground. They afterwards directed their ſtrength againſt ſimilar houſes in the city, deſtroying every thing in them; leaving nothing but the bare walls. Nor, was the young man unſought for. He, was obliged to fly from a place, whoſe court of juſtice had upon a liberal trial, acquitted him of the charge. Had he been taken, he certainly could not have ſuffered long under their tortures; for death would have put an end to his pains. The governor, mayor, and public officers of the city, have been active upon the occaſion: a troop of horſe was called out, and all good citizens invited to rally round the ſtandard of the laws. The mob has ſubſided. But not before the miſchief was done, which they intended to effect.

What a lamentable thing it is, that this ſcourge will ſometimes ariſe, to the terror of all

all good citizens: in the open defiance of laws, and shaking the foundations of life, and of property. They are in government similar to the convulsive throws of nature, which spread an universal alarm. Were the actors in those scenes, conscious of the injury which they do themselves, and their families, waving that which is done the community at large; they would shudder at the part which they had taken, when they reflected upon the example which had been given. They would perceive that the assistance which they had rendered in committing acts of enormity against others; was the direct way of exposing themselves to a like retaliation. They would perceive, that in those violences, they had broken the bonds of government; and reduced themselves to a state of nature. Where, life, liberty and property; are only secure, in proportion to the strength of him who is attacked, and the weakness of his opponent. Nothing is more volatile, nothing more sudden or more violent in their operations, than the progress of the human passions. They are like fire, which begins with a

spark

spark: but neglected, rolls over our heads in a flame. And what can be worse, than the paſſions of an unreſtrained mob? They, may be directed to as many different objects, as there are individuals, who compoſe it. Each one has his revenge, or enmity to gratify; rebellious to the laws, to the peace of their country, they ſtep forth, unreſtrained by any thing but an overmatch of power. And in this, are too often the inſtruments of deſigning men, of bad characters, and more deſperate fortunes.

CAN they anſwer for the iſſue of their enterprize? Can they ſay, thus far thou troubled ſea, ſhalt thou go; and no farther? Alas! they are deceived. And are not brought to a ſenſe of their ſituation, until perhaps ruin ſtares them in the face; and tyranny and deſpotiſm, trample upon their liberties.

Is a government bad? Let it be amended. Are public officers unjuſt, or diſhoneſt? Let them

them be removed, and better ones fubftituted in their place. Are juries partial ? Try them and punifh them. Are citizens aggrieved? Let them feek redrefs, according to the laws of their country. Let reafon, and remonftrance be the fprings of action on the occafion ; and not paffion, malice or revenge. The effect will be happy. It will give fatisfaction to the difcontented, and pleafure to the hearts of reflection.

I HAVE been hindered from making my intended expedition from hence to the lakes, which I regret exceedingly : having thereby loft the fight of fome of the fineft country in the world. Nor, has that been my only mortification. I have been deprived of going to Philadelphia, and of meeting there with characters, whom it was my delign to know. Of once more feeing the man, who is the favorite of America. Believe me, the fcourge of Heaven has been upon that unfortunate city: twenty thoufand of its inhabitants are faid to have left

it :

it: and too many, have taken an eternal adieu! There,

"——————————. *The sullen door,*
Yet uninfected, on its cautious hinge
Fearing to turn, abhors Society:
Dependants, friends, relations, love himself,
Savaged by woe, forget the tender tie,
The sweet engagement of the feeling heart.
But vain their selfish care: the circling sky,
The wide enlivening air, is full of fate:
And, struck by turns, in solitary pangs
They fall, unbless'd, untended, and unmourn'd."

But I am informed the disorder decreases: And the citizens begin to recall their exiled confidence. The approach of winter, seems already to correct the influence of the disease; and to present them with brighter prospects. Commerce, with cautious approaches, begins to resume her sway: and the hopes of returning health, to chase away their fears.

LETTER

LETTER XI.

The public mind much agitated, in confequence of Mr. Genet's proceedings. Strictures upon his conduct.

New-York, November 4th, 1793.

THE public mind has been kept here in continual agitation fince the 22d of the laft month, by the conduct of the French minifter: who feems determined, that if we do not with a good appetite partake of the difh of politics which he fets before us; he will *from his pure regard* to *our* interefts, cram them down the throats of American citizens.

FROM the time of his departure from Philadelphia in Auguft laft, and the publications which about that period took place, refpecting the appeal which it was faid he threatened making to the people from the Prefident's decifions,

fions, he had been tolerably quiet. It was to the receipt of a letter from general Moultrie requesting an explanation of that business, that he was indebted for the opportunity of stepping forth immediately into action; an occasion he did not fail to improve. Accordingly, a letter which perhaps had only been intended as a private correspondence with him; came forth to the public view, as an official requisition from the governor of South-Carolina: accompanied at the same time, with his official answer.

This, immediately became the subject of consideration. With the known friends of America, who had braved the hardships of the late war in conspicuous stations, and still enjoyed the confidence of government; Mr. Genet's answer received universal reprehension. It was approved of, or apologized for by none, but those, whose hearts led them to favor the French revolution; while they did not develope the artifices, contained in all the ministers proceedings: Or by those persons, whose
greatest

greateſt pleaſure is when obloquy can be caſt upon the federal government: becauſe intereſt, diſappointment, and in many inſtances deluſion, have principled them againſt it. And that there are ſuch men, eager to catch every convulſion of government, and to improve it for their own private advantage, under the cloak of the public good; is what the page of hiſtory often ſhews us; and what experience in the preſent times, clearly ſpreads to our view.

The public ferment had not yet ſubſided, when another production of Mr. Genet's miſchievous compoſition appeared in print: ſerving no other purpoſe than to rouſe the public indignation againſt his improper interference. It was his anſwer to the Preſident's proclamation of the 10th of October, diſmiſſing the Sieur Antoine Charbonet Duplaine, from the functions, powers, and privileges of vice-vice-conſul of the French republic. He " having under color of his office commit- " ted ſundry encroachments and infractions on
the

"the laws of the land: and particularly hav
" ing caused a vessel to be rescued with an arm-
" ed force out of the custody of an officer of
" justice, who had arrested the same by pro-
" cess from his court."* By which answer in
his letter to the secretary of state, he said,
He hastened to declare he did not acknowledge its validity. Because the constitution
of

N O T E.

* I was at Boston when the vessel was rescued out of the custody of the marshal, the case was nearly this. A vessel had been brought into that port as a prize by a small French privateer, which was supposed to be an illegal one; according to the construction of the 'Rules adopted by the President of the United States,' transmitted to the different collectors by the secretary of the treasury. The marshal was therefore directed to serve a process upon her, but was opposed; and the vessel was ordered under the guns of the Concorde frigate, then lying in the harbour. And although remonstrances were earnestly made to the consul, it was not until several days thereafter, that she was given up to the marshal. Perhaps it would not have been then done, had not capt. Van Dogen deemed it necessary to sail from Boston in the Concorde: thereby no longer affording protection to the vessel.

of the United States had not given the President the right, which he now appears desirous to exercife." Such, was the ground work of his anfwer, or we may call it his counter-proclamation.

These productions of Mr. Genet, may be viewed as epitomes of his political principles: and may be confidered under two heads. Firft, a fincere defire which he has, of making us take an active part with France, againft the combined powers of Europe; whether it fhould be for our interefts or not. And in cafe he fhould fail to effectuate that immediately, with the confent of the federal government; he fecondly, is inceffantly in all his publications playing upon the paffions and prejudices of the people at large; thereby fowing a jealoufy amongft them with regard to our public officers, to weaken the finews of government, and indirectly effectuate thofe plans, which have openly been defeated. They, have been the refult of reflection no doubt; although I cannot fay of

cool

cool reflection. In them, we find writings wound up with moſt artful cunning; where ſophiſtry, ſentiments of liberty, enthuſiaſm, oblique attacks againſt public officers, and even againſt government, fill up a picture; where, the lights and ſhades are ſo nicely blended, as neither to ſhew where the one ends, or the other begins. This, is the line of conduct of a man ſent over here, as miniſter of a beloved and reſpected nation! For whoſe ſucceſs in the preſent ſtruggle for liberty, wiſhes are daily offered up to Heaven from all America.

WARM from France as a republican, he landed on our peaceful ſhores; welcomed by the plaudits of their inhabitants. Their hearts, ignorant of court politics or intriguing machinations, directed them to lead him by the hand of friendſhip to their abodes. They loved him, becauſe they loved his country. And every where, they indulged the effuſions of their patriotiſm. Such, were the ſentiments universally

universally entertained respecting him; which ha I he but known in what manner to have used, he would still have enjoyed. But buoyed up with the addresses to him, which announced the good wishes of the people to the cause in which he was engaged: he forgot what should have been the object of his mission, as respecting America. He forgot, that it was her friendship which he was to insure: while, he was led away with the hope of involving her in a war.

The tendency of this line of conduct, and of these sentiments disseminated through the medium of a press; at length, appeared with alarming symptoms. For although the people themselves had not been appealed to in opposition against the government; yet the appeal had been made to their gratitude, to their generosity, and to their fears. Or why was the correspondence of a foreigner obtruded upon the public. and that in some instances, before the letters written by him could have reached their deftination?* It muft have been for the exprefs purpofe of having an influence with American citizens, tending to favor the defigns which he nourifhed. And an influence it certainly had: for privateers were fitted out under French commiffions, in American harbours: and many American citizens, fetting at nought the Prefident's proclamation enjoining a neutrality, openly enlifted in the fervice of France. The judicial power was exerted, to ftop the growing evil. Henfield was tried, and acquitted: and cards of invitation were fent by the minifter to individuals, inviting them to dinner with citizen Henfield. No one can believe that this pointed attention to a man who had been charged for a difobedience to the laws of his country, could proceed from perfonal regard: it

N O T E.

* In his correfpondence with Gen. Moultrie, his letter in anfwer, bears date the 15th October 1793. And the whole of the correfpondence was publifhed at New-York, October 22d, 1793.

it was an unbecoming joy, and triumph, which at that moment brought him forward in direct oppofition to the wifhes of the federal government. And which from that moment, completely forfeited the confidence and efteem which had been extended towards him, by American citizens. For from that time, we may date the retrogade of his career ; and follow him in the dereliction of the favor of government.†

AND here, we are at a lofs which moft to obferve, his ignorance of the characters with whom he had to contend; or his effrontery in oppofing himfelf to a phalanx of cool decided oppofition. For to one of thefe caufes, muft be

N O T E.

† Mr. Jefferfon's letter as fecretary of ftate, to Mr. Morris the American minifter in France, directing him to infift upon the recal of Mr. Genet, bears date as early as the 16th Auguft, 1793.

be afcribed the perfevering obftinacy, which has marked, and ftill continues to mark, the fteps of this political character.

LET his inftructions be what they may, however full, or however impofing upon his actions: fhould he be fo trammelled by them, as to be allowed no will of his own; but to be obliged by all means in his power to fulfil them: although in having thus acted, he may ftand juftified to his own country; yet he is entitled to nothing, but the indignation of every true American. Perfectly unjuftifiable, and equally reprehenfible, for improperly interfering in our domeftic government, and endeavouring by every art to lead us into a war, he appears not the friend, but the enemy of our country.

IF Mr. Genet conceived, that the name of *liberty* in America had fuch a majic effect as to open an immediate avenue *for his fchemes* to
the

the hearts of her people; how egregiously I
hope has he been mistaken. Liberty is certainly dear to them. They fought for it, they deserved it, and they have received it. They
know its excellencies—and it is because they
have this knowledge, and wish to retain its advantages, that they have not entered so warmly
into his wishes: or brandished the flag of war,
in defiance of prudence and reflection. With
them, the time of revolution is over. Without the shock of nations, or the intrigues of
court politicians; they have made, and now
enjoy, the most free, and best organized government in the universe—Property, liberty,
and life, are secured by its laws: agriculture,
commerce, and plenty, are enjoyed by its industry. Genius is encouraged: and every honor is attainable to those who deserve them.—
How then he could suppose, that people thus
knowing their happy situation, would assist his
nation beyond what they were actually bound
to do by treaty: how it could ever enter his
head that they would be thus forgetful of their
situation, or of the character of Americans,

which it is high time they should support among themselves, is real'y surprising. Nothing but his enthusiasm can be his excuse. And what is that enthusiasm? It is in the breast of man like the electrical fluid; capable of being directed to the *best*, or most *unhappy* purposes. It is that spirit which is the life of all revolutions. It is that which led American soldiers bare-footed, hungry, and unpaid, to crush tyranny, and to plant the laurels of freedom. But it often has been the means of misleading many by the counsels of intriguing and wicked men. Who have thereby satisfied their individual revenge, by connecting it with the great cause of the nation. It is what has protected, or made a mere nullity of the laws of a country: as thereby good inclinations have been directed by the virtuous, or the wicked. With the first, they have joined enthusiasm to reason; with the latter, it has been the companion of folly and destruction. Under this cloak for all actions, perverse men accuse even virtue herself, of aristocracy, that they may trample upon her with impunity: and adorn
crimes

crimes with the names of democracy, that they may be allowed to commit them. Thus, they disgrace the noblest of all causes, those of *the people*, and *of liberty*. *

How far the enthusiasm which directed Mr. Genet's conduct in this his favorite pursuit, has been engrafted into American systems, witness the President's proclamation of neutrality; approved by the citizens of America†. Can his present conduct then proceed from misinformation

N O T E S.

* ' Aujourd'hui ces pervers aristocratisent la vertu " même, pour la fouler aux pieds. Ils democratisent le " crime, pour avoir le droit de le commettre : et c'est ainsi " qu'ils dishonnorent la plus belle des causes, celle du peu- " ple et de la liberté." in a speech of monsieur Vergniaud, to the national assembly of France.

† Since writing the above, the President's proclamation has been approved by both houses of Congress ; as having been wife and expedient.

R

mation? It were idle to suppose so. He cannot be unacquainted with a determination which is officially and solemnly published to the world. He must then, act thus from *design*. And that, more under its present complexion, of gratifying his spleen; than to serve the interests of his country. It cannot be to strengthen the chain of friendship with her. For, were that his object; he is toiling to a direct frustration of his ends. He is vilifying, and blaming by innuendo's and equivocal expressions, the most beloved and respected character in the union. Else, why charge *some of America's antient friends with indifference?* why charge them with *falsehoods?* Why arraign certain officers of the federal government with *intentions both destructive of liberty, and favorable to our enemies?* Why declare that their *tameness, their small measures in the common danger, which menaces free nations, did not appear to him to be consistent with the sentiments of their fellow citizens, with the true interests of their country?* Why express *his grief at seeing General Washington, that celebrated hero of liberty accessible to* men, *whose schemes could only darken his glory?* Why, charge *the President with exercising an illegal right of dismissing the vice-conful at Boston from his office?* Why throw out the threat *that this becomes a cause of war?* Why cast away the instruction and guidance of the best civilians‡ whom the world has produced; vilify them as hired jurisprudists, and rely only upon the fundamental points of *our* liberty, and that of *his* country, and upon the rights of man *as being engraven in his memory, in characters not to be effaced, and enclosed in his breast with the sources of life?* Why use this language? More, the

child

N O T E.

‡ " I do not recollect what the worm eaten writings of *Grotius, Puffendorf,* and *Vattel* fay on this subject. I thank God I have forgot what these hired jurisprudists have written upon the rights of nations, at a period when they were all enchained. But the fundamental points of your liberty, and our own, are engraven in my memory in characters not to be effaced, and the Rights of Man are enclosed in my breast with the source of life." Mr. Genet's letter of the 27th October, 1793, to the Secretary of State.

child of an heated imagination ; than the cool reflection of a diplomatic character‖ ? But to burst the hands of all law and order; and to fan the embers of a wild enthusiasm—which, although suited to effect revolutions, and to accomplish arduous enterprizes ; is not adapted to support good government. Which, he would have us believe is the mother of all virtue, and of all abilities. And which, from the breast of ignorance or folly, can in his opinion give rife to a knowledge of the fundamental points of liberty, and the rights of man : as the attrition of steel strikes out the latent fire, from the body of a flint.

When this man is observed, continuing this political rant, charging government with a
tameness

N O T E.

‖ All these expressions may be found in his letter to the President of the 13th August : his letter to governor Moultrie. And that to the secretary of state.

tameness and small measures, in the common danger which menaces free nations. When he tells General Washington, that he has not penetration enough to choose those who should be his advisers. When we see him patronizing clubs and societies, throughout the United States; endeavouring thereby to extend his influence, and to support his tottering character§

Is

N O T E.

§ "By a very singular fatality, the representatives of
'the republic in America, are agents of the traitors whom
'she has punished. The brother in law of Brissot is con-
'sul general with the United States from France: Another
'man, Genet, sent by Le Brun and Brissot, with the
'charge of plenipotentiary agent, resides also at Phila-
'delphia, and has faithfully fulfilled their designs and in-
'structions. He has endeavoured to irritate the Ameri-
'can government against us, and has made proposals to
'them equally contrary to the interests of both nations.
'By a very remarkable contrast, while those who sent him
'to America persecuted at Paris the popular societies, and
'denounced as anarchists the Jacobins courageously strug-
'gling against tyranny: Genet, at Philadelphia, made
himself

Is there one American who doth not feel his soul roused in just indignation against this meddler in our councils, and stranger to our soil? Is there one, enjoying the rights of man, who does not feel his liberties encroached upon; and that by foreign influence? Bold enough to interfere with the branches of government, and to dictate what they should observe! Without at once making him know the ground, upon which he stands; and the tenderness, with which he should tread. Without bringing quickly to his recollection, the respect which he owes to a country, equally sovereign with his own; and equally jealous of her rights and privileges. And in fine, without offering up every wish, and making every honest exertion for the recall of one, whose enthusiasm

‘himself the chief of a club there, and never ceased to
‘ make and excite motions equally injurious and perplexing
‘ to government.’——Citizen Robespierre's report in the name of the committee of public welfare, to the national convention of France, respecting the political situation of the republic in November 1793.

enthusiasm has broken the reins of reason and of prudence; and whose actions are continually affronting a government with insults, with which, his nation wishes to be in the strictest amity? If these were not the true opinions to be entertained respecting his measures, in vain have we fought for liberty and independence. We may pursue them: but like phantoms they will elude, and for ever disappoint our expectations. Shackled by the politics of others, and led away by the gaudy colors which they spread, we cannot be said to be free or independent. For power of *will* and *action* is essential to the being so. Without them, we are but the mere instruments of others designs: or the unfortunate dupes, of our own credulity.

Persons are too apt, not to discriminate between *men*, and *things*. As the love which Americans had for France, was at once transferred to her minister; so, if he doth not haste to act with prudence, or his country doth not immediately recal him; the dislike which is now

entertained

entertained against him, may be transferred to his country. And may not be withdrawn, until after she has smarted under its effects. It is thus, that the human passions proceed; which, when wound up to an high tone, embrace all connected to the principal with the love or hatred, which, is entertained for him. When war is inevitable, and the subject is fairly brought, absolutely to be considered, what part shall be taken by America; she must lean to the side of liberty: for she acknowledges no other influence upon earth. But until that happens, I apprehend it is the part of every citizen to respect his own situation: *and to attend to the interests of his country.* Firm, in this line of conduct, he will be unshaken by the arts of faction; and unawed by the threats of power. Reason, will have a just ascendency over his actions; and happiness, in all probability will crown his pursuits.

F I N I S.